The Ambiguities of Dependence
in
South Africa

The Ambiguities of Dependence in South Africa

in South Africa

Class, Nationalism, and the State in Twentieth-Century Natal

Shula Marks

Ravan Press   Johannesburg

Published (Southern Africa) by Ravan Press (Pty) Ltd
P O Box 31134, Braamfontein, 2017 South Africa

First impression 1986

Design: New Art
Set in 10 on 12pt Sabon/Symposia by Opus 61

ISBN 0 86975 282 0

Printed by Galvin and Sales (Pty) Ltd, Cape Town

Contents

Preface

This volume had its origins in a series of three lectures originally given to the Atlantic History Seminar at the Johns Hopkins University in April 1982. I was invited to talk about the ambiguities of dependence — the title of an article I had written in 1974 on John Dube of Natal, frequently described as "the Booker T. Washington of South Africa."[1] I must confess that when Professor David Cohen first suggested I go back to that title, I was a little hesitant. The phrase had seemed a happy one when I started work on John Dube and the politics of Natal, but I was aware even then that this phrase could cover so much of human behaviour, especially the behaviour of politicians, and feared it may have outgrown its utility. Nevertheless, once I began writing I found that the term *ambiguity* did cover — with some ambiguity and poetic licence — the terrain I wished to explore in relation to the nature of the state, nationalism, class, and class consciousness in early twentieth-century Natal.

I say "with some ambiguity and poetic licence" because I use the term *ambiguity* in this book to cover two distinct but related phenomena: ambiguity of meaning and structural ambiguity, for which the term *contradiction* would be equally, if not more, appropriate. Ambiguity in meaning, I suggest, arises not infrequently from structural contradiction or structural ambiguity. Though I do not attempt to vie with the late William Empson in delineating seven types of ambiguity, the word does seem to me to have some of the same utility for historians as for literary critics — by choosing to look at episodes that are on the surface puzzling, we are forced into "teasing out the meanings of the text."[2] As in poetry, so in history, ambiguity serves to alert the reader to the relationship between things. I have written elsewhere that historians should be able to write in chords, for our medium distorts our intentions by its linear imperatives.[3] For ease of explication we separate out what rightly belongs together and can only be understood as a "total" picture. Normally we can only say one thing at a time. Ambiguity however, enables us to operate at several levels simultaneously.

A number of friends and scholars have generously commented on this text, both before and after it had been presented as a set of lectures. In particular, I would like to thank David Cohen for persuading me to give the lectures in the first place and for his support and encouragement thereafter. His perceptive remarks on the lectures and on the draft manuscript disconcertingly opened up avenues in my material I had not been aware of. At an early stage, Lewis Kornhauser allowed himself to be used as a sounding board and gave more assistance than he probably realized. Richard Rathbone clarified my thought and the manuscript by lengthening my bibliography and shortening my sentences. Like Richard Rathbone, Michael Burawoy, Baruch Hirson, Kennel Jackson, Gavin Kitching, John Lonsdale, Alf Lüdtke, Andrew Roberts, Richard Roberts, Stanley Trapido, Leroy Vail, Brian Willan, and Marcia Wright have all made valuable comments, most of which I have tried to incorporate — though on occasion they counselled a perfection I have been unable to attain. Various members of my family offered assistance and advice at different times and tolerated my absences and enthusiasms with admirable fortitude. Symposia in New York and Bad Homburg, and seminars in London, York, and Oxford, afforded a further opportunity to try out some of my ideas before different audiences, and I would like to thank their organizers and participants as well as members of the audience at Johns Hopkins for helping refine and modify my original ideas.

Despite its slender size, this volume has been constructed out of work in libraries and archives in three continents, over many years, and was financed partly by travel funds provided by the Hayter Award and overseas study leave support from the School of Oriental and African Studies, University of London, for which I am grateful. It is also impossible to thank all the archival and library staff who helped me along the way. The assistants in the Natal archives, and in particular Graham Dominy, were, however, outstandingly helpful. I should also like to pay tribute to the indefatigability of the staff at the Killie Campbell Library in Durban, the manuscript collections at the Universities of Cape Town and the Witwatersrand, and the Institute of Commonwealth Studies in London, who did more than their fair share of chasing about to find elusive sources, recalcitrant footnotes, and possible illustrations. Finally I am grateful to Gill Berning of the Local History Museum in Durban, and Annica van Gijlswijk at UNISA, for finding additional, invaluable photographs at a fairly late stage in the preparation of this text.

Introduction

In all societies, new classes and productive forces grow out of the old. In colonial societies, in which new classes are frequently fashioned by external agencies before older hierarchies have disappeared, there is often an articulation of the new capitalist mode of production with older forms of production, class and property relations, political authority, and ideology. Given both the continuities and the disjunctures, the contradictory nature of people's actions reflects a social order that is itself contradictory. The working of the "colonial misunderstanding" means that the words and actions of individuals are both deliberately and accidentally ambiguous, as the colonized don the mask of deference before their conquerors, and conquerors assume the garb of authority before the subjugated. At the psychosocial level, domination is both experienced as ambiguous and elicits ambiguous behavior. Yet the ambiguity of ideology and behavior of individuals arises not simply out of personal psychology but also from their structurally dependent position within the colonial political economy and the colonial state, and the contradictory nature of the colonial order itself. As Neville Hogan has remarked, "Ideologicial ambiguities arise out of structural ambiguities and cannot be explained at the level of ideology alone. Ideology is not self-explanatory. When it is treated as though it were, the result is a moralizing psychologism. Under such an historiographical regime ideological inconsistencies become betrayals, and ideological shifts hypocrisy."[1]

Throughout the essays in this book the metaphor of the mask recurs, in part a metaphor for irony and ambiguity. Both were and are essential to survival in a colonial situation. The black consciousness leader, Steve Biko, put the case for the mask starkly and bitterly in an important essay in 1971: "Powerlessness breeds a race of beggars who smile at the enemy and swear at him in the sanctity of their toilets; who shout 'Baas' [Boss] willingly during the day and call the white man a dog in their buses as they go home. . . . The concept of fear is at the heart of this two-faced behaviour on the part of the conquered blacks."[2] Yet for the historian it is as difficult to detect as it is important to acknowledge the presence of the mask, lest we mistake form for substance and take quiescence for acquiescence.

Like the mask, the tightrope also recurs as a metaphor in this text. And like the mask it expresses the tensions at the heart of colonial society. Max Gluckman describes social structure in Zululand in the 1930s as "a functioning unit, in temporary equilibrium."[3] The tightrope hints at the precariousness of this equilibrium, if indeed it can be described as "equilibrium" at all. The clash between institutions and expectations, the conflict between both classes and cultures, and the wholly disproportionate power relationships inherent in the colonial situation constantly threatened any putative "balance."

The changing nature of domination lies at the heart of these essays on South African society. And a concept of ambiguity is crucial to any understanding of domination; even while demanding obedience, and provoking resistance, domination operates not simply through coercion but also through concessions that themselves are shaped by the nature of resistance. These in turn become the basis of consent as well as of further struggle by the dominated. It is in this light that I try to interpret the nature and effect of policies of segregation in South Africa in the first three decades of the century.

For a North American audience, the term *segregation* (unlike, perhaps, *ambiguity*) may have a familiar ring. The United

States, like South Africa, has had its policies of segregation, and at roughly the same time. Comparisons between race relations in South Africa and the American South have had a long history. Already by the first decades of this century, observers, both black and white, were agreed that "the two societies were traveling along the same road toward a much more competitive and troubled racial system," even if the American South was "miles ahead."[4] More recently the similarities — and differences — have received systematic and scholarly attention. The burgeoning of a new South African historiography, itself influenced in part by radical American reinterpretations of slavery, race relations, and the frontier, has in turn led a number of American scholars to reassess interpretations of race relations in the United States.[5]

Thus, the imperial historian John Cell has taken as his comparative focus segregation in South Africa and the American South between 1890 and 1925, much the same period that is dealt with in this volume. Drawing heavily on the seminal work of Martin Legassick on liberalism and segregation in South Africa, and more generally on the recent South African historiography of class and race, his object is to "compare the evolving matrix of race and class relations in two societies that are widely regarded as being the most pervasively racist in the world, South Africa and the southern United States." His definition of segregation as "an interlocking system of economic institutions, social practices and customs, political power, law and ideology, all of which function both as means and as ends in one group's efforts to keep another . . . in their place within a society that is becoming unified" goes beyond notions of unequal treatment to underlying power relations.[6]

Cell argues that both in the southern United States and in South Africa segregation, which needs to be distinguished from "the broader ethos of white supremacy," was an essentially new set of institutions of social control that developed to cope with the strains of "capitalism, industrialisation, urbanisation and modern state formation."[7] The changes wrought both in the

American South and in South Africa by capitalist development created the need for an overarching ideology of control that could disguise white class divisions while containing black class protest. Neither an atavistic hangover from the frontier or slavery, nor "the crude irrational prejudice of ignorant 'rednecks,'" segregation was the ideology of "well-educated and comparatively moderate men as an apparently attractive alternative to more extreme forms of white supremacy."[8] Nor was it simply a system of coercion; in both South Africa and the Southern United States, it offered "a basis for collaboration that the harder, more inflexible forms of white supremacy could never have allowed."[9]

There were intricate intellectual networks connecting the two societies, not only between the white ideologues of segregation like Jesse Jones, the Phelps Stokes Fund, and the American Board of Missions on the one hand and the Natal educationalist C. T. Loram and the writer M. S. Evans on the other, but also through the resonance of black American experience with that in South Africa, whether mediated through John Dube and Booker T. Washington, or the Industrial and Commercial Workers' Union (ICU) and Garveyism.[10] Nowhere was the transatlantic connection more strongly felt than in Natal, where American missionaries had been at work since the 1830s, and where elements of segregationist policies were in evidence well before the end of the nineteenth century.

Fascinating as the comparisons and connections are between the two societies, we must nonetheless be wary. As the American historian George Frederickson has warned us, the term *segregation* "masks different ideologies and practices":

> Despite some resemblances in practice and a good deal of similarity in ideology and spirit, the institutional foundations and socio-economic implications of the pattern of social discrimination and political exclusion that is usually summed up by the term "Jim Crow" differed substantially from those of "native segregation"

and apartheid. Indeed, the differences are of such a degree as to cast doubt on the value of a detailed comparison of the unequal treatment of southern blacks during the Jim Crow era and the lot of Africans under segregation.[11]

Thus, in South Africa segregation serves not simply as the institutional and ideological buttress of the white monopoly of power at a time of rapid social change; it is the central mechanism for the reproduction of cheap and coercible migrant labor. By emphasizing the urban aspects of segregation and the similarities in the preoccupations of middle-class ideologues, as well as of the black intelligentsias, which are common perhaps to both situations, one may miss the profound significance of segregation as a set of policies in South Africa that links rural labor reservoirs controlled through "precapitalist" social relations and capitalist enterprise through the flow of migrant labor from the countryside.

Moreover, while in both the southern United States and South Africa the anxieties unleashed by capitalist development and rapid social change can be seen to lie at the heart of segregationist policies, the forms that capitalist development took in the two societies differed fundamentally. In South Africa, capitalism had to come to terms not with the fragmented cultures of slaves, but with, in many instances, the still pulsating remains of powerful African kingdoms. The structures and social relationships of African precapitalist society profoundly shaped the struggles that actually crystallized in policies of segregation. The contests over the form and pace of proletarianization took place at a bewildering number of levels: between capital and labor, between and within branches of the state, between different capitalist interests, and between all of these and the precolonial ruling class of chiefs and headmen in the countryside, as well as between the latter and their subjects.[12]

If the segregationist policies of the South African state form the backdrop of this volume, the individual essays are focused around three other themes: the ambiguity of the state, the ambiguity of nationalism, and the ambiguity of class and class consciousness. Each has been shaped around an episode in the life of an individual: Solomon ka Dinuzulu, scion of the Zulu royal house, son and heir to the last Zulu monarch, whose position was recognized by his people, but not — officially at any rate — by the South African state; John Langalibalele Dube, third generation Christian and epitome of the "new African," founder of the Ohlange Industrial School, newspaper editor and first president in 1912 of the South African Native National Congress (which later became the African National Congress); and Allison Wessels George Champion, politician, a leader of the ICU (the largest trade-union organization amongst blacks in South Africa until recent times), executive member of the African National Congress, city-boss, and entrepreneur extraordinary. Between them, Dube and Champion dominated Natal African politics until Dube's death in 1946; Champion continued as an influential and controversial figure in Natal until his death in 1974. Their longevity may well have "enabled them to become magnets for the coteries of interests around them" and have contributed towards some of their "ambiguity."[13] At least in part, the apparent changes in the politics of both these men, which scholars have explained in terms of shifts from "radical" youth to "conservative" old age, can be explained by the changing context of their lives. What seemed radical in the 1900s or 1920s was no longer so in the 1940s or 1950s. I have, however, chosen to look in detail at the period in each of their lives when they intersected with Solomon, whose anomalous position as a king who was not a king provides the pivot around which the ambiguities of state, nation, and class can be organized and explored. In a short conclusion I look at that most profoundly ambiguous figure of all, Chief Mangosuthu Gatsha Buthelezi, who unites in one person the ambiguities of all three. Like Solomon, Dube, and Champion, Buthelezi is a master of the "politics of the tightrope."

In each case the essay starts off with a kind of riddle: in the first, why it is that Solomon was not deposed for behavior that would have caused a lesser chief's instant dismissal. Not only did he insult the governor-general of South Africa in front of an assembled crowd of 6,000; more generally his drunken and dissolute behavior threatened tumult in the countryside as his agents attempted to restore his finances by commandeering cattle from an already impoverished peasantry. The second essay revolves around the move of John Dube from leading spokesman of the pan – South African westernized intelligentsia to stalwart of Zulu ethnic nationalism, who appealed to the South African government to recognize the paramountcy of the Zulu king. And finally the third essay attempts to explain why A.W.G. Champion was banished from Natal not, as has usually been assumed, for instigating the beer hall riots of 1929 or even as a result of his leadership of the ICU, but because of police reports that he was forging an alliance with Solomon ka Dinuzulu — on the face of it an extremely unlikely alliance, as Solomon had been among Champion's arch opponents only a few years before.

In retrospect, these essays were originally written in this way in part as a result of a certain dissatisfaction with much of the existing literature on South Africa in the twentieth century. On the one hand, recent work on the political economy has been marked by a heavy structuralism that has left little space for the role of the individual, and on the other, studies of particular nationalist and trade union organizations have tended to be heavily institutional and have dealt with individuals only at a generalized and ideological level.[14] Moreover, despite the emphasis on the coercive nature of the South African state and the record of black resistance to it — and I would certainly not wish to dissent from either appreciation — important aspects seem to have been left out of the analyses. Despite lip service to the need to move beyond a notion of blacks simply as victims of an all-powerful state, there has been little attempt in the recent literature on twentieth-century South Africa to show the struggles waged by men and women against their oppression or indeed the ways in which they "have become accomplices in their own sub-jection."[15] Thus the role that the so-called black dominated classes — as much dominated in the structuralist texts as their authors see them in reality — have played in shaping the nature of the segregationist South African state has been largely ignored even in the best and most recent accounts of the period.[16]

There are welcome signs that this is now changing. Within the last few years, Charles van Onselen's graphic portrayal of the Witwatersrand between 1886 and 1914; the richly textured essays on rural society by Stanley Trapido, Colin Bundy, William Beinart, and Peter Delius; the remarkable achievements of the Witwatersrand History Workshop guided by Belinda Bozzoli; Brian Willan's outstanding biography of Sol. T. Plaatje; and Dave Hemson's important study of Durban dockworkers have all textured and nuanced and, at times, transformed our under-standing. Without their work and comradeship, this book could not have been written.[17]

What these essays attempt to do is bring together in some sense the insights we have gained from both the new social history and the structural marxism of the seventies, by looking both at in-dividual agency and social constraints. This undoubtedly raises its own problems. Moreover, by using a moment in the life of the individual to exemplify broader historical processes, some of what is unique to his or her biography can get lost. And by trying to draw out the totality from a micro-study, some of the dynamics behind the structures may evade examination. The method does however seem to enable us to move beyond an approach that Geoffrey Barraclough has characterized as "an almost neurotic absorption with questions of motivation"[18] on the one hand, and a structural determinism that leaves no space for human agency on the other. It leaves room for a social history that takes account of class-based relations of power.[19]

Despite the tendency both in the structuralist literature and in

some social history to discount "events," these essays unashamed-
ly center around events. These are not grand events like the
French Revolution or the English Civil War, it is true; rather,
they are the kind of "specific, bounded happening" usually
associated with anthropology. Perhaps in dealing with
Zululand-Natal, I was subconsciously influenced by Max
Gluckman's classic *Analysis of a Social Situation in Modern
Zululand*,[20] based on field research completed in 1938, only a
few years after the episode I discuss in Chapter 1. There seem to
be echoes in Solomon's encounter with the Earl of Athlone in
Gluckman's brilliant and famous description of the opening of
the bridge in Zululand in 1937, though I hope I move beyond its
functionalism even if I cannot vie with the intimate detail of his
field research and the vividness of his eye-witness account.

To return to the event is not to escape the need to "recover the
texture of daily life in the past,"[21] but to recognize that part of
that texture is only recoverable through certain kinds of events.
It is to recognize, with Philip Abrams, that "the adequate
'unpacking' of an event requires meticulous attention to both
action and structure and, if the connection between them is to be
seized, precludes a one-sided assertion of either."[22]

It is precisely this connection between what Abrams calls
"action and structure" that I hope to capture, by bringing
together structure and process, process and meaning, meaning
and motivation. With Abrams I believe that at the heart of social
analysis is the problem of human agency or what he calls "the
problematic of structuring," and what E. P. Thompson has
hauntingly termed "the crucial ambivalence of our human
presence in our own history, part subjects, part objects, the
voluntary agents of our own involuntary determinations."[23] As
Abrams puts it:

> The problem of agency is the problem of finding a way of accounting
> for human experience which recognizes simultaneously and in equal
> measure that history and society are made by constant and more or less

purposeful individual action *and* that individual action, however
purposeful, is made by history and society. How do we, as active
subjects, make a world of objects which then, as it were, become
subjects making us their objects? It is the problem of individual
and society, consciousness and being, action and structure. . . .
People make their own history — but only under definite circumstances and conditions: we act through a world of rules which our
action creates, breaks and renews — we are creatures of rules, the rules
are our creations: we make our own world — the world confronts us
as an implacable and autonomous system of social facts.[24]

It is through the specific institutions of time and space that larger
structures become a lived reality and are reproduced; it is in "the
small segments of society . . . [that] experiences are forged."[25]
Hence I focus on Natal-Zululand, and on three individuals at a
particular moment in time. The "problem of structuring,"
however, means that a return to the local and individual cannot
absolve us from a regional as well as a national and indeed an
international perspective. Over recent years, historians and social
scientists have agonized over their "unit of study." Yet as the
noted Dutch historian Jan Huizinga remarked in 1934, "Every
historical fact opens immediately to infinity." More important
than the starting point is the way in which this point "opens to
infinity," the way in which the local and the particular are
located within a wider context, and in turn enable us to refine
our understanding of that wider context. Natal, the smallest and
least politically influential of the four provinces of what became
the Union of South Africa in 1910, cannot be understood outside the broader changes in southern Africa in the nineteenth and
twentieth centuries. Twentieth-century South Africa is better
understood after we have contemplated Solomon in his confrontation with the governor-general.

In the nineteenth century, Natal was a British colony; for much
of the century, Zululand was an independent kingdom. Yet from
the beginnings of colonial settlement in the region, white settlers

and, increasingly, black peasants were locked into the world economy. Sugar production from the 1860s, based on Indian indentured labor, made the movements in prices and labor markets of crucial concern to capital, the colonial state, and workers alike. With the Cape Colony, Natal controlled the inland trade, and this meant that even in the nineteenth century, the colony's interests were closely tied to those of her neighbors as well as dependent on the world economy. For much of the nineteenth century, Natal's sugar barons were dependent on the vast flow of Indian indentured labor to the mines and plantations of the British Empire, which was the origin of South Africa's contemporary Indian population.[26] With the discovery of diamonds in Griqualand West in 1868 and in 1886 of vast seams of underground gold on the Witwatersrand, deep in the interior of South Africa, Natal became even more affected by the ups and downs of capital accumulation in the region as a whole.

It is arguable whether the colony could be said to have boasted an independent ruling class for most of the nineteenth century. Until the grant of self-government in 1893, the dominant alliance of absentee landlords linked with merchant capital and sugar-planters constituted a stratum of the imperial bourgeoisie, and not a particularly powerful one at that, although it was sufficiently strong to induce the British government to allow the indenturing of Indians to resolve the labor problems of the sugar planters while leaving the rents of the landlords intact. Their leverage in political terms was weak. For the brief period of self-government between 1893 and 1910 local settlers achieved a greater degree of control over their destiny; the state they created differed in quite material ways from the colonial state. Even then, in the final analysis, they relied on the imperial connection to bail the colony out in the event of serious trouble. With Natal's reluctant political incorporation into the Union of South Africa in 1910, the relationship between the local dominant group of settlers and the central state was in some ways analogous to the relationship of slaveholders in the American South to the North:

Natal was embedded in a national system in which the settlers shared power unequally with a far more powerful northern bourgeoisie, and one opposed moreover to the continued importation of Indian labor.

The conflict between Natal and the central state was not simply a matter of differing ruling class traditions and style, although much has been made of this on various occasions through the twentieth century as Natal has threatened to "take-off"[27] — to secede from the Union. Nor was it simply that Natal was the most "British" of the four colonies that made up the Union, or even that Natal was the one part of South Africa with a major plantation sector based on indentured Indian labor, though this was important. The discord also grew from conflict between the demands for labor within Natal, despite the presence of the large Indian population there and the propensity of the gold-mining industry and other ancillary economic activities on the Rand to siphon off what the Natal bourgeoisie regarded as their African labor. By comparison with the Rand, the undercapitalized sugar plantations and coal mines of Natal offered lower wages and considerably poorer conditions, as central government health and labor inspectors ceaselessly pointed out.[28]

The partial replacement and partial incorporation of the local state and bourgeoisie by the central South African state and national bourgeoisie, with their different economic imperatives and strategies of domination, lies behind some of the ambiguities discussed in Chapter 1. In Chapters 2 and 3, the location of the African intelligentsia and workers in this wider context again partly explains the contradictory quality of belief and action. At the most mundane level, both Dube and Champion had direct personal experience of the national stage. As in many parts of the colonial world, it was the weak African intelligentsia — themselves a product of Christianity, colonialism, and the demands the colonial state and mission churches made for literate clerks and functionaries — who first became conscious of themselves as a class on a national stage. Small in number and without the backing of a powerful bourgeoisie, they were both the most ardent believers in the new colonial order and its most vociferous critics. The second essay, then, is devoted to the contradictions within nationalism itself and between it and ethnic nationalism, as well as to the structural ambiguities of the intelligentsia.

If, after 1910, the Natal bourgeoisie became part of a national bourgeoisie, African workers had long been part of a regional labor market. While the different practices of colonial rule in the various colonies and republics of South Africa in the nineteenth century continued to influence local institutions into the twentieth century, in important ways the experience of migrant workers was one of constant movement across the frontiers established by history and geography. From the 1870s Africans from Natal were present in considerable numbers on the diamond fields at Kimberley, and by the 1890s they were joined on the Rand by increasing numbers of workers from Zululand. Those who did not make their way to the Rand were to be found in the kitchens and factories, and on the roads and at the harbors of Durban, which already by the end of the nineteenth century was South Africa's second most important port. And because South Africa's industrialization developed upon the basis of a migrant labor system, the daily lives and consciousness of workers and peasants — usually the same people in this period — were inexorably shaped by both rural homestead and capitalist enterprise, whether mine-compound, sugar plantation, dockyard or factory.

To experience the full disciplining effects of the national and indeed international labor and commodity markets, the rigors of the work place, and the rituals of entry into it, Africans did not necessarily have to move across the boundaries that separated town from countryside, or province from province. For labor-tenants and farm workers were equally shaped by the realities of accumulation in a peripheral economy, and in Natal, a doubly peripheral economy. Their experience of white domination, like that of the migrants to town, was both more direct and less mediated than back in the "reserve," and they spread their knowledge of white power through the rural areas. Migrant workers in Durban and labor-tenants in the countryside were, as we shall see, George Champion's constituency, and it is through the contradictory nature of their experience that the answer to the "riddle" posed by his deportation in 1930 should be sought.

Despite the constant interplay between the specificities of the local and the general, it nonetheless seems to me worth looking in detail at the Natal end of the story. In Natal, the contrasts between theory and practice, between exploitation, expropriation, and political suppression of Africans on the one hand, and the ideology of separate development, trusteeship, and paternalism on the other, have been particularly marked. A colony that probably experienced the most concentrated missionary effort in Africa, Natal has also been the scene, for more than a hundred years, of the most sophisticated attempts to rule through "traditional authorities." The patterns of African responses have matched these ambiguities to the present day. Ambiguity has been the price of survival in a contradictory world.

1. *Solomon ka Dinuzulu and attendant, 1920s*
(South African Government Archives, Cape Town).

2. 3.

4.

2. *The Earl of Athlone in
South Africa*
(South African Government
Archives, Cape Town).

3. *Dinuzulu (seated) with his
sons, Solomon and David,
in Middelburg c.1912*
(South African Government
Archives, Cape Town).

4. *The Shaka Memorial at
Stanger, unveiled by Solomon
ka Dinuzulu in 1932*
(Killie Campbell Library).

CHAPTER 1

The Drunken King
and the Nature of the State

On 24 July 1930 the governor-general of South Africa, the Earl of Athlone, visited Eshowe, the administrative headquarters of Zululand, a largely African territory that had been conquered by the British in 1879, annexed as a Crown Colony after nearly a decade of civil war, taken over by the settlers of Natal in 1897, and then incorporated with it into the Union of South Africa in 1910. All the chiefs and their followers were ordered to attend the occasion, one dear to the heart of colonial administrators and intended to impress the "native mind" with the power and wisdom of their authority through the appropriate ceremonial and words of warning.[1] Forty-eight chiefs and over a hundred headmen were seated before the podium from which the governor-general was to address the multitude; behind them in a semicircle were massed some six thousand of their followers.[2] After the majority of the crowd had assembled, Solomon ka Dinuzulu, son of the last Zulu king, arrived at the head of a chiefly motorcade. Then, to quote the words of the official report, "the first incident occurred." Solomon wished the vehicles to be parked in line and was reluctant to leave his car

---

This title is a shameless plagiarism of Luc de Heusch's famous *The Drunken King or, the Origin of the State*, translated and annotated by Roy Willis (Bloomington, 1982; originally published as *Le roi ivre ou l'origine de l'Etat*, Paris, 1972). The similarity between the two works ends here.

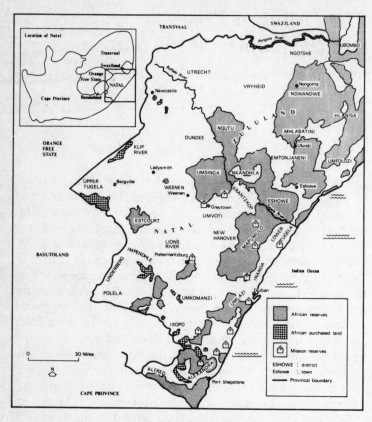

Natal and Zululand, c. 1910.

and take his place at the center of the chairs provided for the chiefs. Eventually taking his place among them, he pointed his finger in the face of one of the local officials and remarked loudly:

> You are doing a bad thing here. What right have you to all these people? I am the king of this country. . . . What do you mean by turning the king of this country into a dog.[3]

Solomon followed this up, according to the highly indignant Native Commissioner and magistrate of Eshowe, with "the most positive illustration of what is known in the army as 'dumb insolence'."[4] When the Chief Native Commissioner engaged him in conversation Solomon "deliberately" remained in a reclining position; while the governor-general was addressing the meeting he "repeatedly turned around and carried on conversations with his fellow-chiefs"; when the governor-general made statements with which he disagreed, he visibly showed his disapproval by shaking his head. Clearly most shocking was the fact that he reserved his most vigorous disagreement for the following: "In your Chief Native Commissioner and in your Native Commissioners you have men to look after your welfare and to give you their best advice. Go to them with your troubles and difficulties."[5] What particularly incensed the local Europeans, however, was Solomon's speech by way of reply:

> It is a pleasure for me to welcome you here for I am also a person of royal blood. The people at my back recognise me as a Chief of the Royal House of Zulus. Each country has its own King. We are loyal to the King of England but he has many countries to rule and it is difficult to understand how he can administer them all. Some people think they can rule a country by their cleverness but we know that only people of Royal Blood are fitted to rule. Things in this country will never be right until I am recognised as the head of the country. It is regretted that you visit us only at the close of your term of office. However, we wish you God-speed. We trust you will convey to the Royal Family in England the

unsatisfactory treatment meted out to the Natives of this country.
Farewell.[6]

To add insult to injury, at the close of the meeting Solomon,
who had earlier been asked to lead in the rendering of the royal
salute "Bayete" and refused on the grounds that he was the only
one entitled to it, remained seated while the Zulu were ordered
to hail the governor-general three times. To the consternation of
those local whites who understood Zulu, the assembled crowd
roared not "Bayete" but the vaguely threatening substitute
"Bayeza" ("they come").[7] Solomon then left the meeting before
the governor-general — to greetings of "Bayete" as he moved
through the crowd.

A buzz of outrage amongst local officials and settlers followed
this scene. They demanded immediate action. "The evil effect of
this man's conduct cannot be too strongly emphasized,"
fulminated the Eshowe magistrate. "If no action is taken against
Solomon the authority of the Native Commissioners will be
impaired."[8]

Memoranda flew between the local officials and the Chief
Native Commissioner in Pietermaritzburg (the administrative
center of Natal) and between Pietermaritzburg and the Native
Affairs Department in Pretoria. The governor-general met
Solomon at Nongoma — regarded by the Zulu royal family as
the true capital of Zululand — and proffered words of fatherly
advice, reprimand, and condescension. Solomon was swift to
offer his apologies, aware at least from the newspapers of the stir
he had caused. On 11 August he wrote to the resident magistrate
at Nongoma (it was a rule of "native administration" in Natal
that all communications to government had to be addressed by
Africans through their local magistrate) in response to a letter
informing him of the government's disfavor and even more
ominously withdrawing his liquor permit:

This matter does not treat me well. . . . For my part I do not remember any offence of it whether I spoke unsuitable words before the Governor-General at Eshowe as I was drunk as you say and I spoke in Zulu and I was interpreted for in English. I would very much like to hear my offence. . . . This, father, startles me very much that I should be pounced on with a letter like this. I wish you would explain to me thoroughly my offence which I committed in Eshowe. I say this because it injured my good name, therefore I see this matter is a very serious one because to destroy the head is as though the body were dead also. . . . Therefore I say you should have called me and explained to me thoroughly as my father who is over me and with whom we live here at Nongoma.[9]

After due consideration the government decided to withhold half Solomon's annual stipend of £500. The Chief Native Commissioner was left to break the unpleasant news at Nongoma, but in private, in order, as he put it, "to show that the Government is not angry but grieved, and that what has been done is in the nature of correction rather than punishment" for Solomon's having appeared at the meeting under the influence of alcohol. The commissioner also took the opportunity of suggesting to the chief that the government also "viewed with disfavour" his recent visit to the Durban headquarters of the African trade union movement, the Industrial and Commercial Workers' Union, and a meeting with its by-this-time notorious leader, A.W.G. Champion.[10] Indeed in police circles in Natal this encounter was regarded as far more ominous than Solomon's original offense.[11]

That the administration should have been somewhat concerned at the reports of Solomon's behavior was perhaps not surprising. This was not the first time he had been accused of premeditated rudeness before a royal guest, of deliberately using a state-made royal event to boost his own authority.[12] An even more spectacular episode of this kind occurred in 1925 when the Prince of Wales had met nearly 50,000 Zulu assembled in Eshowe. On that occasion, too, Solomon's behavior outraged local settlers and was the matter of adverse comment — so much so that he sued the local newspaper, *Natal Mercury*, for libel. At the time he was alleged to have been deliberately rude to the Prince of Wales, by arriving late at the afternoon's dances, and of having in premeditated fashion encouraged the Zulu to greet him rather than the Prince, disturbing the dignity of the occasion. Local officials, who felt that their handling of the ceremony was under question, sprang to the chief's defense. Solomon won his libel suit, and there can be little doubt that the episode was worked up by elements in Zululand who were opposed to any indication that the Zulu king held a position of authority in the territory.[13]

Solomon's confrontations with British royalty are not simply further examples of the ways in which colonial regimes manipulated the notions of "imperial monarchy" to legitimate their rule. They also serve to illuminate the contradictory and many-layered nature of *herrschaft*[14] in early twentieth-century Zululand. At their most obvious both encounters were of course ambiguous. Despite the libel verdict in Solomon's favor, there can be little doubt that in 1925 Solomon was greeted with very widespread popular acclaim and almost certainly used the occasion of the British royal visit to boost his own position. His subtlety went well beyond that of the local officials, who were surprised to find that not only had he personally equipped a hunting expedition to East Africa to procure a magnificent pair of ivory tusks to be presented on behalf of the Zulu nation, but that he had also prepared a fine present and illuminated address of his own for the Prince. These were gestures the administration could not decently stop, but they were hardly as innocent as the local magistrate maintained: "There was nothing political. It was just a young man's proper expression of humility, loyalty and honour."[15]

Having had to defend their position on Solomon in 1927, the administration's allegation of drunkenness in 1930 may well have been a convenient fiction for Solomon and the administra-

tion alike. There is no doubt but that Solomon drank heavily —
as had his father before him — and that he was a man of uncer-
tain temper. Personally he was under very considerable stress.
Already seriously ill (he was to die less than three years later at
not more than forty years of age), he was in deep financial
trouble, while his domestic life — if the testimony of his first
wife is to be believed — was in considerable disarray.[16] According to local officials Solomon was "very obviously under the
influence of alcohol" and "in a cantankerous frame of mind"
well before the afternoon's ceremonies.[17]

How relevant is this, however? Although in general over the
years Solomon had adopted a path of caution with local
officialdom — as his artfully obsequious letter to the magistrate
of Nongoma indicates — there is after all substance in the phrase
in vino veritas. Were his words not a truer reflection of his feelings when emboldened with its effects than when threatened
with its deprivation? When playing to an audience of 6,000
potential followers than when writing to a paternalistic official
in private? George Heaton Nicholls, a leading sugar planter and
M.P. for Zululand,[18] who had his own reasons for making light
of the episode, took a somewhat less serious view than the
majority of settlers and officials. "Solomon," he wrote, "was
slightly intoxicated and not quite so respectful in his speech as he
might have been . . . though he was perfectly logical and
coherent in what he said. . . ."[19]

The ambiguities, however, go well beyond the rights and
wrongs of the libel suit, Solomon's drunkenness, whether feigned
or exaggerated, or his mask of abject apology and deference to
the magistrate of Nongoma. They are rooted in the nature of
herrschaft in twentieth-century Zululand and the ambiguous
position of Solomon as son and heir to Dinuzulu ka Cetshwayo,
the last independent Zulu king; they are rooted both in his
tortured relationship with the Natal administration and in his
complex relationship with Zulu peasants and workers, landowners and professionals, each with their own expectations of

the monarchy.

The origins of the Zulu kingdom in a series of wars amongst Africans in northern Natal-Zululand in the second and third decades of the nineteenth century are relatively well known, although the reasons for the kingdom's rise are still a matter of some controversy. Between 1818 and 1828, Shaka Zulu established a powerful centralized state, based on the enlistment of the young men from his own and the conquered chiefdoms into regiments. These formed the basis of a highly successful army that gave Shaka a monopoly of force and could be directed both internally and externally. He used it systematically to remove any alternative focus of ideological, political, or economic power. In addition, the regiments gave the king a source of surplus labor, which could be used both to extend the cultivation of the royal fields and in raiding and herding cattle. By deciding when the soldiers could marry and by allocating the cattle for their bridewealth, the king controlled not simply family life and demographic increase, but also the totality of productive and reproductive relations in the society.

Like most of the societies of southern Africa even before the rise of Shaka, the Nguni societies of Natal and Zululand had long passed from any simple agricultural self-sufficiency or kinship-based political organization to more complex social formations. Based on mixed agriculture (sorghum and, probably from the eighteenth century on, maize were the staple crops) and pastoralism, and with relatively simple technology, production was characterized by the absence of private property — though each homestead had stable usufruct rights over the land allocated to it for cultivation by the chief — and by the division of labor both between the sexes and between chiefs and commoners.

Although agricultural production for subsistence was undertaken mainly within individual homesteads grouped in kin-based villages, cooperation between homesteads and villages was crucial for the production of the surplus necessary to maintain the chiefly class, and for the system of exogamous marriage practised by the Nguni. Through their overall control of village production, as well as of bridewealth, chiefs ensured the continuity of social and economic life. They made the major decisions regarding planting, harvesting, and consumption, and they controlled the long-distance trade from the coast, which from the eighteenth century began to transform social relationships in the region.[20]

As in other parts of Africa, kinship underpinned the relations of production and reproduction and provided their legitimating ideology; the chief was seen as "father of the people" and was responsible, at least in principle, for ensuring the redistribution of surplus to the old and frail. With the rise of the Shakan kingdom, the Zulu king took over the powers of the lesser chiefs and their ideological positions. He, too, was "the father of the people," and earlier norms of redistribution served both to legitimate and to constrain the king's powers of surplus extraction. Elaborate ceremonial and ritual bolstered his extensive powers and reinforced the mystical powers of kingship. These in turn derived from the special position the king held in relation to the ancestors, with whom he could intercede on his people's behalf in order to ensure the continuity of the social order and its well-being. As a result, Max Gluckman has written,

> The social cohesion of the Zulu state . . . centred in all particulars on the king. His rule was sanctioned by the force behind him, but he was supposed to use it to defend the national interests: the tyrants who abused it, were ultimately deposed. The unity of the system was derived from more than force. As the symbol of national unity and health, the king was magically treated in the first fruits ceremonies that the nation might prosper and conquer its enemies, home and foreign. He stood as final judge who was bound . . . to defend legal rules which helped control Zulu social and ecological relations. For Zulu moral values stood the King, not only the symbol of social cohesion but also its artificer.[21]

There were of course incipient cleavages within this society, if not fully fledged class divisions: between men and women, between elders and juniors, and between the aristocracy, the Zulu royal family, the subordinate chiefs, and the commoners. The incorporation of Zululand into the labor and commodity markets of southern Africa in the second half of the nineteenth century and the moment of conquest and colonial annexation between 1879 and 1889 had contradictory effects on these cleavages. On the one hand the fact of conquest masked earlier divisions, and on the other, the way was opened up for those who wished to escape the constraints of the kingdom, for whatever reason. This had already happened to some extent after the establishment of the first white settlement at Port Natal in the 1820s, with the flight of refugees to the haven provided by the traders, and more importantly after the arrival of the missionaries who followed less than a decade later.

Before 1887 and the annexation of Zululand, the scale of this outward movement was small. The establishment first of an Afrikaner republic then of a British colony in Natal south of the Tugela River deprived the king of a substantial section of his territory and control over a large number of subjects, but in his now more constricted domain he continued to hold sway over a largely self-sufficient political economy. Indeed, it can be argued that it was the relative self-sufficiency of the Zulu kingdom that led to its conquest by Britain in 1879. Behind the imperial conquest was the need to release the manpower tied up in the Zulu regimental system for the insatiable labor market that developed in South Africa in the wake of the mineral discoveries in the last third of the century.[22]

Yet conquest did not mean outright proletarianization either here or in most of the rest of southern Africa. In many ways the colonial order actually bolstered the power of African chiefs (though not the Zulu king) against their subjects, as they became the local agents of colonialism as tax-collectors, labor recruiters, and administrators of customary law. Even south of the Tugela, in the territory Shaka's successor was forced to cede to the incoming whites, the early settlers were unable to transform the indigenous people into a wage-earning proletariat. In the case of the Afrikaner Voortrekkers, they had neither the will nor the capacity to do so; and even the later British settlers were far too weak in numbers and capital to restructure African society in so far-reaching a fashion without massive assistance from the British state — assistance that the mid-Victorian treasury was unwilling to provide.

To some extent, Shaka's economic transformations had laid the basis for the replacement of the Zulu tributary state by the new colonial state in Natal. Homesteads still rendered up their surplus product through subordinate chiefs and homestead heads, but now to colonial authorities instead of to Shaka's tribute-collectors. Imperial decision-making about Natal was dominated by absentee landowners linked with merchant capital. They were happy to extract rent from African producers while they waited for the stream of white immigration that would bring about a rise in land prices. Their interests thus co-incided with the imperatives of administrators anxious to avoid the open conflict with Africans that would have resulted had there been an attempt at direct expropriation. Thus, when in 1860 sugar was successfully exploited for the first time, there was no readily available supply of labor. Africans still retained a hold on the basic means of production, land and cattle, even outside of the reserves specifically allocated for their occupation between 1846 and 1864 and could earn the colonial taxation or rent through cash-crop production. And the numbers of whites in the colony were far too small to sustain plantation agriculture, even had the planters been prepared to use free wage labor. The solution adopted by the sugar planters and the colonial state was to import large quantities of indentured Indian labor and to bring in a certain amount of migrant Tsonga labor from southern Mozambique.

All this in turn reinforced the tendency of the authorities to conserve African societies in Natal, and in part explains why Natal's policies in the nineteenth century provided precedents for aspects of South Africa's twentieth-century segregationist policies: the allocation of reserved lands for African tribal occupation, the codification of "customary" law, administration through acceptable authorities, the exemption of Christian Africans from customary law, and the attempt to prevent large-scale African urbanization through the institution of a system of labor registration. In nineteenth-century Natal to an even greater extent than in twentieth-century South Africa, colonists were forced to come to terms with the strength of precapitalist social formations and then attempt to utilize elements within them for their own purposes of surplus extraction and control. In Natal in the nineteenth century this was received in the form of rent, tribute, and some labor tax; in South Africa in the twentieth century more directly in the form of labor power.[23]

In Zululand, too, there were constraints on the power of the colonial state or capital to simply restructure African society in accord with immediate self-interest, despite the fact that here colonial rule followed a far more spectacular act of conquest and half a decade of civil war. Although conquest and annexation meant that the labor power of young men, formerly available for utilization by the Zulu state, was now available for the mines, industries, farms and plantations of the Transvaal and Natal, the administration had first to satisfy two major concerns: to find the means to pay for its own survival and to maintain local stability at the lowest possible cost. This in turn meant ensuring that the hut tax earned outside the territory was remitted back home. It led to an alliance similar to that in other parts of southern Africa between chiefs and administration for ensuring the continued control of the homestead and the homestead head over the labor power of young men. At the center of this was the continued hold that chiefs and homestead heads had over bridewealth and thus marriage and homestead formation. The so-called recognition of "native law" under the Shepstone system in Zululand — and this is true also of Natal — "was not just a veneer covering total subordination." It was based on "a shrewd understanding of the distribution of power in precolonial Nguni societies and the way in which this could be utilised by the colonial state."[24]

In both Natal and Zululand, then, control and the extraction of surplus — whether in terms of rent, tribute, tax, or labor power — were premised on the utilization of the powers of the chiefs and the homestead heads who became the subordinate agents of the state. The Zulu king posed a problem of an entirely different order, however. In Zululand, as in colonial states all over Africa, the existence of a centralized kingdom offered advantages and dangers. Once conquered, the successful co-option of the existing ruling class — one accustomed, moreover, to exacting tribute — could lighten the burdens of a hard-pressed and thinly manned colonial service. At the same time, the king provided an alternative focus of power. At the pivot of the local power structure, his *herrschaft* was backed not only by an earlier coercive capacity — the regiments of young men who formerly constituted the army and rendered tribute in labor to the king — which the colonial authorities could not fully control, but also by the political and ideological hegemony that the Zulu royal family had successfully established in the course of the nineteenth century. For the settlers of Natal, vastly out-numbered by the potential proletariat on their frontiers, the dangers posed always outweighed the potential advantages. While imperial officials and later the Union's Native Affairs Department could stand aloof and attempt to manipulate the undoubted and continued hegemony of the king for their own purposes, the settlers, whether in Zululand itself or in the neigh-boring territories of Natal and the Transvaal (a section of which was carved out of Zululand in 1884 and incorporated into Natal in 1904), were only too acutely aware of their own weakness and the continued power of the king. For them the major obstacle to capitalist expansion was the Zulu king, the obvious rallying point for any resistance to the expropriation of land and labor.

Precisely because he expressed the unity of the people, and because he had first call on their surplus, the opening up of Zululand to capitalist penetration was seen to be dependent on the king's removal. As an African remarked when Dinuzulu, Solomon's father, was exiled for the second time on charges of high treason in 1908, without their king "the Zulu people would be like coolies."[25] During the Anglo-Zulu War of 1879, British propaganda was devoted to showing that the removal of the despotic and tyrannical king, the head of a mighty "man-slaying machine," would be in the best interests of the people themselves. Yet attempts after the war to replace the monarch by chiefs disloyal to him erupted in a series of bitter civil wars, which ended in the direct annexation of the kingdom as a British colony.[26] Continued unrest led in 1887 to the arrest and trial for treason of Dinuzulu, Cetshwayo's son and successor, and his immediate followers. They were sentenced to ten years' exile on St. Helena. It is no coincidence that hut tax was collected for the first time in Zululand in that year, nor that 1889 saw the first major exodus of migrant labor from Zululand to the mines and farms of Natal and the Transvaal. By the 1890s Zululand was fully locked into the colonial economy of southern Africa, and by 1887 the British government was firmly convinced that Dinuzulu could be safely returned to Natal as chief of the immediate followers of his father, the Usuthu in the Nongoma district, and a potential government ally. The reluctant settlers were appeased only by the simultaneous imperial handover of the territory to Natal, and promises that the king would have no recognized jurisdiction further afield.[27]

The situation was almost impossible, and immediately rumors were heard that Dinuzulu aimed to rebuild the powers of the Zulu kings. As the Commissioner for Native Affairs later put it, "Contrary to his instructions, he began to build up a 'pageantry of royalty'; men were enrolled into regiments as under the old regimes, and Native women were drawn from all parts of the country to form his harem. The Usutu kraal became a place of intrigue and a place of refuge for all those fleeing from authority."[28]

The blood-curdling fantasies of white colonists, at a time when primitive accumulation in Natal was proceeding apace and bringing settlers into direct confrontation with the African population in a new way, mingled with the wishful dreams of once independent Africans who were increasingly aware of colonial encroachment on their land and labor. It made a heady mixture, which exploded in parts of Zululand and Natal in the so-called Poll Tax or Bambatha Rebellion of 1906, an uprising that was in some sense the result of self-fulfilling prophecy by the settlers, and the last armed resistance to proletarianization on the part of Africans. After this, Africans did not need to be reminded of the white man's power. Although in Zululand "proper" the uprising only affected the south, where the exactions of landlords and the experience of proletarianization had gone furthest, the sheer scale of the punitive action was no doubt sufficient to deter others from confronting maxim guns and dum-dum bullets with spears and assegais, both then and for a long time after. In 1906, about 24 whites lost their lives in a variety of ways, not all of them in combat, and 37 were wounded. The exchange was far from equal: between 3,000 and 4,000 Africans had been killed and some 7,000 taken prisoner. According to the *Times of Zululand*, a newspaper not prone to be disturbed by settler savagery, about 700 Africans had had their backs lashed to ribbons and 4,700 sentences including flogging had been carried out before the government itself put an end to this "judicial violence" in 1908, under prompting from the Colonial Office and the British governor. In 1907, 1 in 400 of the total male adult population was flogged, almost all of whom were black; this excluded juvenile offenders who were birched. In the same year, 1 in 37 of the total African population was in prison some part of the year, 1 in 19 of the total male population.[29]

At the end of 1907, Dinuzulu, whom the settlers were convinced had instigated the entire uprising, was arrested and tried on twenty-three counts of treason. Found guilty on three, he was exiled for a second time and ended his days in the Middelburg district of the Transvaal, where he died in 1913.[30] The odds against the Africans then were very clear. The "Bambatha Rebellion," whatever its causes and whoever the participants, was clearly a crucial moment in the establishment of colonial *herrschaft*. The basis for settler accumulation had been laid. Significantly, again, it was after Dinuzulu's second exile that planters were able to take over the lands in Zululand that had been delimited for white occupation five years earlier.[31]

Solomon, with appropriate symbolism, was born during Dinuzulu's first exile on St. Helena. From the moment of his birth, he shared in the dilemmas confronting his father. For Solomon, growing up in the shadow of Dinuzulu's double exile and the Bambatha massacre, ambiguity was the essence of survival. His royal birth could not protect him from physical and verbal racist assaults by whites[32] while it ensured that he was the center of almost constant intrigue both within the Zulu royal family and from its traditional enemies.[33] On more than one occasion, attempts were made on his life.[34] Named by his father Nkayishana, a Zulu praise name applied to a "spirited, daring, fearless young man," Solomon had constantly to temper his daring with deference.[35] Throughout his life he inhabited the margins of the permissible and the paradoxical, the king who was not a king, who was never more sober than when he was drunk. As Erving Goffman has shown, the mask is not unique to black men and women living in a white dominated world; it is an essential part of "the presentation of self in everyday life."[36] Nevertheless, for Africans the contradictions were undoubtedly starker. Like Booker T. Washington, the ex-slave in the American South, Solomon "was forced from childhood to deceive, to simulate, to wear the mask. With each group of blacks or whites he confronted, he learned to play a different role, wear a different mask."[37]

After Dinuzulu's death what had now become the government of the Union of South Africa had to make a decision about his son and heir. The central government was able to take a somewhat more relaxed attitude than the old Natal authorities. For the Native Affairs Department, the overreactions of local officialdom to the Zulu royal family seemed calculated to precipitate the disorder they most feared. The Cape administrators in charge in the early days of Union in the Department of Native Affairs had never been as close to the threat of Zulu power or as paranoid about its effects. Moreover, the prime minister, General Louis Botha, had been among the Boer buccaneers who assisted Dinuzulu against his enemies in the civil wars of the 1880s (and who had claimed as their reward a huge tract of Zulu territory) and regarded the chief with a certain degree of sympathy. More importantly, the government was rather more concerned with the demands of mining capital for a stable rural base for the reproduction of its labor supply in the reserves and with the demand of the more powerful farmers of the maize belt than with the immediate competition for land and labor in the least politically significant of its provinces. Natal settlers, however, continued to be adamantly and vociferously opposed to any form of recognition for the special position of the Zulu royal family.

In 1916 for example there was one of those flurries of hysteria to which Natal was prone when the support that the Zulu kings enjoyed became manifest. As a result perhaps of a misunderstanding, Solomon had called a ritual hunt to "cleanse the nation" after the period of mourning for Dinuzulu had ended. The Chief Native Commissioner, an old Zululand magistrate, was convinced that this was yet another ploy by the Zulu kings to gain recognition from the people — as indeed it probably was.[38] Only the intervention of the central government prevented the removal of Solomon from Zululand and a heavy fine in cattle being imposed.[39] As late as 1920 the newly appointed Chief Native Commissioner,

C. A. Wheelwright, was most concerned by the visit of Solomon's brother David to Cetshwayo's grave — news of which "thundered through the country."[40] Wheelwright warned the keepers of the grave against "the consequences of continuing to be a hindrance to the government and getting mixed up in political matters. They had a lesson during the rebellion and now they were deliberately courting trouble again by becoming mixed up with royal youngsters."[41]

Not that Wheelwright was unaware of the hold that Solomon had as "direct and representative descendant of the old Zulu dynasty." The fact that it had been "in power until such comparatively recent times [meant] that the mantle of omnipotence successively worn by Tshaka, Mpanda, Dingaan and Cetshwayo is well remembered by the Zulus and the nimbus of which is in the eyes of the Natives still associated to a large degree with Solomon."[42] His solution was to recommend that the government purchase a tract of land for Solomon in the immediate vicinity of the traditional gravesites of the Zulu kings. This would have the dual object of "scotching" any aspirations Solomon might have for wider recognition and reducing the necessity for his moving around the country, while at the same time proving "a potent factor in obtaining and keeping the goodwill of the Usutu party [i.e. the immediate followers of the Zulu royal family] who will then be unable to reproach the Government with neglecting to care for one whom they are pleased to refer to as its 'orphan' and whom they at present describe as 'a wanderer and uncared for.'"[43] Government efforts in this regard were foiled by the total refusal of local farmers to part with the desired land despite their constant litigation against the royal family on these lands to extract rent, and their frustration at the royal refusal to provide tenant-labor for their farms.[44]

In part because of the contradictory strands in formulating policy in relation to Solomon's position, it took four years before he was recognized to have succeeded even to his father's limited position. Yet Botha's words on that occasion were sufficiently tinged with ambiguity to encourage Solomon and his followers to seek further recognition over the next decade and a half:

> I want peace now — rest for the Zulu nation: and if you go back with that purpose — to assist in maintaining peace and good order — then you will become a big man in Zululand.[45]

The compromise was the best Botha could achieve in view of the conflicting demands of the settlers that the royal family be destroyed and the increasing realization on the part of the central government that the royal family had powers that could be used and manipulated by the administration.

Quite manifestly it was not possible for the government to ignore the Zulu royal family, an expedient that had been tried and had failed in the case of Dinuzulu. Wheelwright, who was specifically appointed Chief Native Commissioner as the "new broom" to sweep Natal into line with the central government "native policy," expressed what lay behind the 1916 decision clearly:

> I maintain that the decision arrived at is the best. It has . . . captured the point which so far has been missed by every administrator handling Zululand affairs and hitherto — to wit: confining the [chief's] authority from an executive point of view while at the same time using the incumbent for all such administrative purposes as Government may see fit to call on him to exercise over the whole of Zululand.[46]

The opportunity of so using Solomon arose almost immediately, as the South African government looked to Zululand to improve their recruiting drive among blacks for the South African Native Labour Contingent serving in World War I; indeed the administration quite explicitly linked his recognition to this.[47] Contrary, however, to the colonial expectation that men would immediately be forthcoming for "Solomon need only raise his hand and every able-bodied Zulu in the country will respond,"[48] the African reaction to his recruitment drive was far from enthusiastic. At a meeting of 12,000 men and women called by Solomon at Nongoma, at which his chief adviser and uncle, Mnyaiza, urged the men to be conscripted, he was met with a "rowdy refusal." One brave spirit shouted out, "We are no longer free agents. We belong body and soul to the Gold Mining Companies and the government."[49] According to a report in the *Advertiser*, even the chiefs responded with some acerbity: "We imagined we had been called so that you could point out to us our prince who would know us and him because we have long been living without a leader. . . . On the first occasion of your call . . . you point out the sea to us. Just tell us of any ancestor of ours whose bones are buried overseas. WE WILL NOT GO THERE." The women present also rose in indignant opposition: "We say our children are being taken so that they may be drowned at sea."[50] The men refused to eat the meat provided by Solomon for the occasion and hurled offensive epithets at Mnyaiza.

Although the vehemence of the response undoubtedly owed much to the sinking of the troopship *Mendi*, in March 1917, with the drowning of more than 300 Africans on board, the response also illuminates one of the central ambiguities in Solomon's position. His *herrschaft* was in inverse relation to his recognition by governmental authority. When his dependence on government support became manifest and he began to carry out the behests of the colonial administration in unambiguous fashion, his significance as a focus of resistance both to white rule in general and to the subordinate chiefs, who had largely by this time come to be seen as "the government's boys," was undermined. As the magistrate of Estcourt observed at the time of the Zulu recruitment, "Disloyalty to the government is at the root of the matter and as Solomon has identified himself with the Govt. he is . . . also a casualty of the same disloyalty."[51]

Solomon learned from this experience. His speech before the governor-general, designed for his black rather than his white audience, was in part a recognition of the tightrope he trod. There were limits to collaboration with the government beyond which the king could not go. When, for example, as a result of Solomon's extravagance in the early 1930s the government bailed him out by paying his debts and then imposing a levy on his people, Solomon was aware that there might be opposition.[52] At a meeting intended to defuse the situation, the majority of elders agreed to the levy, but one Titose Ntshangase probably expressed the feelings of many of the commoners when he sounded a note of warning. After recording his gratitude that the government had paid the king's debts, he went on:

> He hoped that the Chief Native Commissioner would keep an eye on Solomon so that such a position would not occur again. He asked the indunas [headmen] to keep an eye on him when he went wrong. The indunas were there as representatives of the Zulu nation, to keep an eye on him and to advise him. . . . The King was subject to the will of the people. Tshaka became powerful through the efforts of his people — not through his own efforts. Most of Solomon's debts were contracted when he left home and visited large centres. Perhaps some of the people would not pay the levy and they would suffer imprisonment. They understood that the government would pay Solomon's debts and the tribe and mealies and now they were asked to carry this extra burden. They wanted the government to look after their child. In ancient times an unworthy king lost his throne at times. . . .[53]

This was an ominous reminder of what had happened to the king's ancestors Shaka and Dingane, who were assassinated when, it was popularly believed, they had overstepped the limits of their people's tolerance.

The preparedness of the government to pay Solomon's debts shortly after his speech at the governor-general's meeting raises a further level of ambiguity in this story. Considering the nature of the offense, there can be little doubt that state action in the case of a lesser chief would have been far more severe. What strikes one about the administrative correspondence and actions at this time is — contrary to the views of the king's supporters like Heaton Nicholls — the forbearance of the state. Throughout his life it would seem that Solomon was able to exact tribute from Zulu in both Natal and the Transvaal. In the northern districts of Ngotshe, Babanango, and Vryheid the magistrate complained of a dual tax structure that was leading Africans to leave the farms in search of additional cash. The amounts involved were considerable: chiefs £5. 10s., Induna and headmen £2, 5s., and commoners £1, 1s. per annum; "and any foreign natives [*sic*] such as Basutos, Shangaans, Blantyres etc., who take unto themselves Zulu concubines, £1/0/0 per annum." Although the payment was "supposed to be purely voluntary . . . there is strong reason for believing that it is regarded by the large majority as an order, and consequently no effort is spared to satisfy the demand."[54]

The establishment, in the early 1920s, of *Inkatha ka Zulu* (see Chapter 2), an organization designed by the Zulu aristocracy and the African petty bourgeoisie to gain state recognition for the king, was in large measure also intended to collect funds for the Zulu royal family under the guise of a general fund for land purchase and general welfare purposes. According to the Chief Native Commissioner, it had placed "considerable sums of money amounting . . . to many thousands of pounds into the pockets of Solomon and his advisors."[55] Nevertheless, by the late 1920s, Solomon's financial affairs were in a state of chaos. He was heavily in debt to the local storekeepers, bottle-store owners, and car dealers, who at a time of world depression were increasingly reluctant to take a tolerant view of his excesses. They began to foreclose on their loans and as they demanded cash, so Solomon's agents intensified their efforts to collect cattle on his — and, it should be added, their own — behalf. Acting in Solomon's name they were able to extort several thousand head of cattle from an already desperately impoverished peasantry. Zululand was in the throes of the second year of severe drought, while in certain areas a malaria epidemic was raging. Food riots in the "royal" districts of Nongoma and Mahlabatini in the following month revealed the gravity of the situation.[56]

Although Solomon's agents' activities extended to parts of the country over which he was supposed to have no jurisdiction, the state initially took no action, though they watched with anxiety. *Inkatha's* fund-raising activities, too, were sanctioned, as the organization was seen as "the most promising counterblast" to the Industrial and Commercial Workers' Union, then making dramatic headway amongst Natal's rural and urban poor. "Under administrative supervision," it was believed, *Inkatha* "might be made a power for the good."[57] When the activities of Solomon's agents jeopardized the precarious stability in the rural areas, impeded tax collection, and threatened Solomon himself with action in the bankruptcy courts, the administration stepped in to save him from total ruin.[58]

Thus, although the state did not actually recognize the paramountcy of the Zulu king and refused to allow Solomon to call on chiefs related to the royal house to assist in paying off the government loan as he demanded, because it once again feared that he might use the opportunity to further his claims of paramountcy, it nevertheless handled him with considerable circumspection. Despite the cries from the majority of Natal settlers and especially from the Afrikaner farmers of the northern districts that the Zulu royal family be removed, the state also followed a course of ambiguity. The contrast with what had happened to Dinuzulu at the beginning of the century is striking. This has to be understood, however, in a wider context than simply that of Natal or Zululand. Everywhere in Africa at this time, British colonial authorities were handling "traditional authorities" with far greater subtlety than at the turn of the century. South Africa was not immune to policies of indirect rule being devised in both West and East Africa, nor to the censure of imperial critics.[59] More importantly, the ideology and practice of "indirect rule" had a decided resonance with the ideology and practice of segregation as it was now being developed in South Africa itself.

In twentieth-century South Africa the lines of domination are stark and brutal. Coercion is undisguised both in its institutions and its ideology.[60] The conquest of African societies in the last third of the nineteenth century was the essential precondition to the development of South Africa's mineral wealth. A nexus of laws and practices — passes controlling movement, migrant labor, closed compounds, and Master and Servants laws making strike action illegal — enabled a system of ruthless capital accumulation based on mining to take place. This in turn fueled South Africa's agrarian and manufacturing "take off." With the creation of the unified South African state in 1910, the vast majority of black South Africans, almost the whole of the working class, were systematically excluded from the incorporative practices of the parliamentary system, and from any share in the possible rewards of capitalist growth.

An ideology of segregation based on color provided the legal framework for domination and its legitimation. For liberal writers, the badge of color had seemed so obviously the basis of this exclusion that the class basis of domination has been ignored, while the overtly coercive practices of the state have seemed so crude and so easy to document, that by and large Africans have been seen as the passive recipients of state policies simply enforced from above.[61]

Martin Legassick was the first to draw attention to the importance of segregation as a set of policies specifically designed to cope with the strains of a society undergoing rapid industrialization. Segregation as a coherent set of policies was initially formulated by the Milner administration during the first decade of the twentieth century and devised to resolve the problems that arose in the wake of the urbanization and increased proletarianization of Africans consequent to the mineral discoveries of the late nineteenth century.[62] More recently, Marian Lacey, in a meticulously detailed analysis of South African "native policy" in the first two decades after Union, has remarked that "one of the most significant acts of the Pact government [i.e. the coalition government of the Labour and Nationalist parties under the premiership of General G.B.M. Hertzog in 1924 – 29] was to insist on a policy of enforced retribalisation based on the Natal system. This meant 'refurbishing' a hybrid traditionalism and recreating tribal authorities who would be directly responsible to the supreme authority of the Native Affairs Department."[53]

Yet segregation was not simply a set of practices of domination imposed from above, by a state rationally resolving the contradictions of rapid social change. Despite the appearance of settler power, the South African state in this period, particularly in the rural areas, was neither as monolithic nor as omnipotent as is often assumed.[64] Alf Lüdtke has recently criticized Marx and Weber for underrating the fact that "the permanent use of *physical violence 'from above,'* executed by state officials, was a necessary condition not only for the establishment, but also for the *continuation* of exploitation, unequal exchange and the institutional reproduction" of capitalism.[65] In the South African case it is difficult to make this mistake. The facts of state violence confront black subjects and constitute their world at every turn. Nevertheless even in South Africa, the state was and is also faced with the need to "manufacture consent" and find agents of control. Although it could and did make use of direct force on occasion — and during the period of primitive accumulation this was particularly marked — military coercion was expensive and potentially dangerous; except in short, sharp bursts state authorities had neither the capacity nor the inclination to indulge in it. It remained an option in the urban areas, where the large concentrations of population and of police made the use of armed force against popular demonstrations a frequent occurrence. Thus, in Durban, as we shall see, where old lines of deference and paternalism were being challenged in a new way in this period, in 1929 and 1930 African workers were directly confronted by armed troops. In the towns, class conflict was both more immediate and more containable through police and military action.

In the rural areas, however, this was far more difficult. Once the basis for colonial domination and accumulation had been laid in the countryside through conquest, more institutionalized forms of *herrschaft* and modes of negotiation had to be sought. The pageantry of a visit by the Prince of Wales or the earl of Athlone we witnessed at the beginning of this essay was part of this attempt. In the late nineteenth century, a powerful battery of laws had been established in Natal to bolster settler domination, but by and large these had to be implemented by the authority of the chiefs. By the second decade of the twentieth century, the resultant discrediting of the chiefs led the state to attempt alternative ways of maintaining control. By the 1930s visits by important state officials had become annual events in the countryside, in which the law was "explained" to assembled chiefs and followers in an attempt to establish hegemony in a segregated and class-divided society. This was never an uncontested hegemony, however. As we have seen in the case of Solomon, there was always the danger that the dominated would capture the state's ceremonies for their own purposes.

The objectives of the new policy of segregation were set out perhaps most explicitly and more broadly in a letter by Heaton Nicholls, who by this time was becoming the most influential spokesman for segregation on Smuts's opposition front-bench:

An adaptionist policy demands as its primary concept the maintenance of chieftaindom [*sic*] without which tribal society cannot exist. The institution is the necessary pivot around which all tribal evolution must take place. . . . The adaptionist policy assumes a difference between the Abantu and the Europeans. It assumes some measure of territorial segregation. It assumes what is in effect the growth of a national consciousness amongst the Abantu themselves [though Nicholls was thinking here more of local ethnic nationalisms than any pan – South African black nationalism]. . . . The opposite policy of assimilation substitutes class for race and if continued on its present basis must lead to the evolution of a native proletariat, inspired by the antagonisms of class war. The process of assimilation has already gone very far and unless some effort is made to stem the tide of tribal disintegration, it will soon be too late.[66]

Paradoxically, Hertzog's policy of "refurbishing" traditionalism in the 1920s, supposedly based on the "Shepstone system", flew in the face of some of Natal's most dearly cherished administrative practices. Thus, the normative Natal system now gaining favour in Pretoria was not without its contradiction when reapplied back home, the result of what Heaton Nicholls termed "the Zulu War and Bambatha mentality."[67] As the governor-general himself pointed out to ministers on his return from the Eshowe meeting:

> I cannot but wonder whether the very policy to which Government is committed . . . — of . . . preserving Tribalism as far as is possible, and of supporting the authority of Chiefs — is not seriously hindered by the failure to use this great capacity for personal devotion and discipline [as manifested in the support for Solomon] instead of trying to suppress it.[68]

Like Heaton Nicholls, Athlone was perturbed by the "revolutionary and subversive influences . . . which are generally summed up in the term 'bolshevism'" "stirring among the Native populations of Southern Africa," and advocated the recognition of Solomon as paramount chief as the only alternative to "the more or less rapid disintegration of the Zulu Nation through the influence of the I.C.U. or kindred organisation."[69]

Yet the attempts both to find an increased role for Solomon — as much undermined by Natal officialdom as by his own extravagant and self-indulgent way of life — and to reconsolidate chiefdoms which had been deliberately broken up after the Bambatha rebellion roused deep anxieties among Natal settlers, convinced once again that the Union government was selling them down the river. The divisions within the state apparatus at local and central level and the opposition of Natal settlers meant that another twenty years elapsed before the Nationalist government felt itself strong enough to impose recognition of the Zulu monarchy on Natal.[70]

CHAPTER 2

John Dube and the Ambiguities of Nationalism

In August 1933 Solomon ka Dinuzulu died. A year of mourning was followed, as is customary among the Zulu, by a great ceremony of purification and cleansing, the *Ihlambo* ceremony. One of South Africa's first anthropologists, Mrs A. W. Hoernle,[1] present at the ceremony by government invitation, recorded her impressions in enthusiastic terms:

> From every clan, from every chieftainship, from all large districts acknowledging the paramountcy of the Zulu chief, there came representatives to take part in this lifting of the Mnyama [the blackness and gloom that engulfs the nation for the year after the king's death]. . . . Men from Pietersburg, Johannesburg and other parts of the Transvaal, men from every corner of Zululand and right away down to the centre of Natal were there, many of them having spent their last sixpence to take part in the gathering of the clans to renew their fealty to their leaders. . . . Early in the morning of Monday August 28th, this vast gathering from eight to ten thousand men dipped their spears or their guns in 'white' medicines which are thought to prevent any accidents during the course of the hunt with which the Ihlambo begins and which is the first great combined action in which men take part to shake off their lethargy and, at the same time, be welded once again into a united body of representatives from every branch of the Zulu people.[2]

There had been no such gathering, no such spectacle, since the death of Mpande, Solomon's great-grandfather, in 1872. Clearly

5. John Langalibalele Dube
(from T. D. Mweli Skota, ed. and comp.,
The African Yearly Register Johannesburg, n.d., c.1931, p.144).

6. *The Ohlange Institute, John Dube's Christian Industrial School*
(From Mweli Skota, *The African Yearly Register*, p.406).

7. *The* amakholwa *community at Edendale Training Institution,*
c.1900. It includes two members of the Msimang family and Simeon
Kambula (top row, standing from left to right, 2nd, 12th and 18th)
and Stephen Mini (2nd row seated, 3rd from the left), all mentioned
in the text (Natal Archives, Pietermaritzburg).

overcome by the "emotional character" of the ceremony, "the sacred religious feelings," the "orderliness and the discipline of the hour-long procedures," and "the most impressive laments . . . in the music of any people,"[3] Mrs Hoernle failed to remark on some of its more mundane, but at the same time equally noteworthy, features. The contrast in official attitude with what had followed Dinuzulu's death could not have been more complete. On that occasion, the Natal authorities would dearly have liked to prevent the entire ceremony; it was only the intervention of the Union Native Affairs Department that allowed a small purification ceremony to take place — amidst much foreboding. When, despite its express prohibition, Solomon held a ritual hunt following the ceremony, as we have seen, it was taken as yet further evidence of the machinations of the royal family to conjure up the support and recognition of their position that was seen as so dangerous by the local settler populace. In 1934, the proceedings were filmed in colour by African Film Productions, Ltd., in the presence of the newly appointed chief native commissioner, as well as of representatives of the sugar industry and Chamber of Mines.[4] Among the key speakers was John L. Dube.[5]

Eulogized by B. W. Vilakazi on his death in 1946 as "the incarnation of the spirit of his age,"[6] Dube was *the* spokesman of the *kholwa* (i.e. African Christian) community. Born in Natal in 1871, the son of the Reverend James Dube, one of the first ordained pastors of the American Zulu mission, he was educated at Inanda and Amanzimtoti Theological School (later Adams College) before accompanying the missionary, W. C. Wilcox, to the United States of America in 1887. There he worked his way through Oberlin College over five years, while supporting himself in a variety of jobs and lecturing on the need for industrial education in Natal. After a brief spell back in Natal, he returned to the United States between 1896 – 1899 for further training and to collect money from American philanthropists for a Zulu industrial school along the lines of the famous Tuskegee Institute established by Booker. T. Washington in Alabama.

In 1901 Dube established his school in the Inanda district, and a couple of years later started the Zulu-English newspaper, *Ilanga lase Natal*. A founding member of the Natal Native Congress in 1901, he was present in 1909 at the meetings of African opponents to the Act of Union, and in 1912 was invited to become the first president of the South African Native Congress (later to become the African National Congress). Though, as we shall see, he was ousted from the presidency in 1917, he continued in a prominent position in the Natal branch of Congress, running it virtually as an independent fief, until his death in 1946. Initially Dube's school at Ohlange (the first purely African-founded and African-run industrial school) and his position as newspaper editor and politician had led white Natalians to regard him as a provocation and a challenge, "a pronounced Ethiopian who ought to be watched";[7] by the time of Solomon's funeral he was established as the revered elder statesman, representative of "responsible native opinion."[8]

Dube's oration at Solomon's funeral was typically double-edged and didactic. After a brief explanation of the ceremonies they were witnessing — presumably for the benefit of the white observers, but perhaps also for younger western-educated blacks, whom he feared were losing knowledge of their traditions and culture — Dube pointedly reminded the white man of his "burden": "I think the white race has a tremendous responsibility to lead us on the right lines. But that leadership must come from the experience of give and take. We have a lot to learn from the white man and he has a lot to learn from us." He concluded, even more pointedly, with "an earnest appeal to the Government to give our chief a status that will place him on a firm foundation to undertake the responsibility of care of his people. . . . We want the head of the Zulu nation to be a Paramount Chief who is so recognised by the Government."[9]

For those familiar with the relationship between Christian and non-Christian Africans in nineteenth-century South Africa, or with recent sociological denunciations of the Christian mission converts as at best "alienated from their roots" and at worst "decultured" or psychologically enslaved,[10] or with the conventional wisdom that John Dube was the Booker T. Washington of South Africa,[11] this demand would seem to require some explanation. Dube's position is at least as puzzling as that of the South African state. In the first chapter we looked at the ambiguities in the relationship between Solomon ka Dinuzulu and the segregationist South African state, which had, on the one hand, to come to terms with a chief "whose descent is such as to command the involuntary respect of the Zulu people"[12] and, on the other, to avoid alienating the local administration and the bulk of white settlers. This chapter deals with the equally paradoxical relationship to Solomon of Natal's Christian African intelligentsia, essentially the more prosperous landowners and peasants as well as the clergy, clerks, interpreters, and teachers, who came to be among the monarchy's most fervent supporters.

In the nineteenth century, as Norman Etherington has shown, the initial converts to Christianity were largely the despised, the disparaged, and the disaffected, drawn to the mission stations by the prospects of land and security. By far the largest category was homeless refugees, the product of the Shakan wars, which ravaged southeast Africa in the nineteenth century in the wake of the rise of the Zulu kingdom.[13] John Dube's father, James, for example, fled as a child with his mother to Daniel Lindley's mission after his father, the Qadi chief, Dube, was killed by Zulu regiments in 1837. As Dube himself put it before an American audience in 1897: "My grandfather was a powerful Zulu chief. He was a reformer and did not agree with Chaka, the leading Zulu king who believed that the only way to have power was always to be on the warpath. . . . I think it was better than being a king, to be a Christian, because Christianity is the greatest civiliser in the world."[14]

Etherington describes well the tense relationship between African society and the new communities of Christians that were, in Natal, established on mission reserve land especially set aside by the colonial state. For many, the mission station marked a fundamental alteration in lifestyle in the aftermath of the early nineteenth-century upheavals. Many of their traditions referred to the anarchy of that period, to the arbitrary quality of authoritarian chiefly rule, to warfare, refugees, hunger. On their stations, the missionaries set out "consciously and actively to promote economic differentiation and the formation of social classes, and the mission stations provided auspiciously positioned vantage points or pioneer columns in this process."[15] Christianity went along with new forms of agricultural production for the market, a transformed ideology towards accumulation, and a readiness to accept the education being proffered by the missionary. The gulf between mid-Victorian norms of mission Christianity and the demands of the Zulu kingdom was particularly deep; until after the Zulu War of 1879, according to Etherington, quite simply "Christianity and Zulu citizenship were mutually exclusive."[16]

In many ways, the converts on the mission stations who responded with such alacrity to the growth of colonial markets, and who saw in education a way into the privileges of colonial society, seemed to the mid-Victorian visitor to embody the ideal of the independent yeoman farmer. As an Anglican clergyman writing of a mission settlement in Natal in 1874 enthused: "There is not a village in England corresponding to Springvale where every man lives under his vine and fig tree."[17] Some of the American Zulu mission settlements and the Wesleyan Methodist stations at Edendale and its various offshoots were far wealthier. By 1864 there were about 600 inhabitants at Edendale with forty-eight upright houses, twenty-two ploughs, fourteen wagons worth ninety pounds each, and twenty spans of oxen of the same value.[18]

To take but a couple of examples: The Reverend Daniel

Msimang, one of the early followers of the Reverend Alison (who had founded the Edendale mission with a group of converts he gathered together in the Orange Free State and brought on an epic journey back to Natal via Swaziland), had two houses on eighty-nine acres at Edendale and large blocks of shares in the syndicate from Edendale that had bought up land at Driefontein and Kleinfontein in the 1860s. His movable property included 2 ploughs, 2 wagons, 36 oxen, 260 goats, and 20 cows.[19] His son, Joel, born at Edendale in 1854, was also a wealthy man. Although he lost 700 head of cattle during the rinderpest epidemic, which decimated cattle herds all over southern Africa in 1896–97 and increased the dependence on wage-labor of most Africans in Natal, he was nonetheless able to apply for permission to purchase two farms in 1916 and to offer to pay for one outright at a cost of £3000, while putting down a mortgage of £4000 on the second.[20] Nor was the Msimang family alone. John Dube's father, although an ordained minister, earned "all but a fraction of his income" from trade and transport riding and his not insubstantial landholdings.[21] As Dube himself put it: "The day my father came into that country [Natal], the good missionary Mr. Lindley, taught him to use a plough, and he became as rich as any white man there."[22] This wealth provided the almost legendary thirty gold sovereigns that enabled the young John to sail for the United States of America in 1887.[23]

For the prosperous peasantry settled on the Protestant mission stations of the Cape and Natal, as for the petty bourgeoisie that derived from it and that in the last third of the nineteenth century was forged out of "a diverse set of regionally and ethnically defined local groupings" into a self-conscious and coherent national bourgeoisie in the new cities of Kimberley and Johannesburg, the mid-Victorian "code-words" *progress* and *improvement* had a material reality.[24] It was out of the mid-Victorian vision of a "progressive world order," based on the virtues of free labor, secure property rights linked to a free market in land and individual tenure, equality before the law, and some notion of "no taxation without representation"[25] that African Christians in the nineteenth century constructed their world.

The South African sociologist, Ben Magubane, is right, of course, to stress that

> the conquest of Africans was not a momentary act of violence which stunned their ancestors and then ended. The physical strength directed against African societies was only the beginning of a process in which the initial act of conquest was buttressed and institutionalised by ideological activities. British hegemony . . . was to saturate the society and its values to the extent that they would become common sense for the people under its sway. It was to be enshrined in a set of meanings and values which would be confirmed by practice.[26]

We have already seen some of these processes at work in the way in which the South African state attempted in the 1920s and 1930s to make use of the Zulu royal family. We must be careful, however, there as here, not to oversimplify. In neither case was the hegemonic ideology simply the invention or imposition of the imperial or colonial ruling class: to be successful it had to pick up, transform and manipulate real elements in the experience of the dominated classes. For this new class of property-owning and aspiring *kholwa*, the moral imperatives of the nineteenth-century bourgeois liberalism and the attack on "traditionalism" both resonated with their own interests and experience and provided a language of resistance. This occurred in much the same way as Eugene Genovese has suggested that when slave revolts became revolutionary and "raise[d] the banner of abolition, they did so within the context of the bourgeois-democratic revolutionary wave, with bourgeois property relations."[27]

On the mission stations in Natal, American Board converts, Anglicans, and Methodists were ardent exponents of the Protestant work ethic and the virtues of private property and individual land tenure, because they had grown as a class out of precisely these institutions. Nor were the outward signs of petty bourgeois class identification lacking. The description by F. R. Statham of a dinner given to the Africans of Driefontein who had fought on the British side during the Anglo-Zulu War of 1879 is doubly revealing, both of the extent to which the *kholwa* identified with the imperial order on whose side they were prepared to fight, and of the social texture of their lives.

> At the native tables the rule of alteration is strictly observed, no two men or women sitting together. At the upper end of the centre table sits young Simeon Kambule, with his future bride beside him . . . with a really pretty mouth and expression, and with her hair done in immense frisette at the back of her head. She is dressed in a pink and white striped muslim, less pretentious than the satins around her, and all the time keeps jealous guard over Simeon's sealskin cap, nursing it on her knee. Opposite Simeon is John Zulu . . . something of a dandy in his way; his black velveteen waistcoat is irreproachable, so also is his white waistcoat, while the crimson sash over his left shoulder is secured by a triple gold ring on his right hip.[28]

A not dissimilar flavor emerges from the description by the American Board secretary C. H. Patton of his visit to the Christian settlement at Groutville and its chief, Martin Luthuli, uncle of the famous Nobel Peace Prize winner Albert Luthuli. The congregation was "not only civilised but educated and prosperous," and the chief "was garbed like a city gentleman, long black coat, starched shirt and all the paraphernalia of civilisation with not a detail omitted, even to the necktie pin. He was a Christian and a highly prosperous man, being the owner of a sugar plantation."[29]

Martin Luthuli, Simeon Kambule (who in 1917 owned 796 acres of land), and the Msimangs were part of a small group of wealthier African landowners in Natal by the turn of the century, and the nucleus of John Dube's constituency. If in the early 1900s there were only some 1,500 individual landowners, with about 102,000 acres between them,[30] the first decade of the century also saw the formation of a considerable number of land syndicates, along the lines established by Edendale and Driefontein in the mid-nineteenth century. According to a representative of the Klip River Agricultural Society in 1917: "Natives will go to [land] sales and buy in such a way that no Europeans will be able to buy. . . . Two hundred may find the money, but only one need buy the farm."[31]

As usual the spokesman for white farming interests exaggerated. The amount of additional land acquired between 1905 and 1916 amounted to little more than 70,000 morgen (147,812 acres), while over the next ten years the operation of the 1913 Lands Act made further land acquisition difficult, if not impossible, and the amount of African-owned land actually dropped.[32] Nevertheless, in 1928 a not unsympathetic farmer wrote to the *Natal Witness*:

> The Native Land Act is the only thing which stands between the European landowners of Natal . . . and the wholesale acquisition in future by natives of lands all over the country. . . . Those who argue that the native can never compete with the white man buying land are deliberately shutting their eyes to what is already taking place. . . . Few people realise the awakening that has taken place among the natives during the last ten years or so. They are fencing their gardens, are using planters and cultivators for their crops, planting fruit trees, building better houses, growing vegetables for the market and in a hundred different directions showing evidence of the rapid germination of a spirit of uplift, which of course is all to the good.[33]

Some of the land being purchased in these years after 1913 (in the areas released under the Act) was bought by syndicates organized by chiefs for communal occupation, the only form of resistance to and protection from outright proletarianization for themselves and their followers: however, the *kholwa* purchasers, even those who formed syndicates, saw this land as a basis for accumulation. In the inimitable words of the Natal Local Native Lands Committee of 1917, "Generally, native purchasers of land are progressive and have aspirations far beyond those of the ordinary native."[34]

The larger landowners were no longer simply peasants employing family labor. Many, like Martin Luthuli, were canegrowers, employing either labor-tenants or wage-labor. Thus, Luthuli, for example, hired what he was pleased to describe as "30 or 40 boys . . . at the same rate of wage paid by Europeans"[35] as *togt*, or daily-paid, casual labor, a process that increased as more of these landowners went over to sugar production in the twenties and thirties.[36]

By the beginning of the twentieth century most of the larger landowners, together with other members of the African *kholwa* elite, were involved in a network of political organizations, vigilance associations, and welfare societies. The most important were the Natal Native Congress and the Exempted Natives Society, which attempted to improve the status of those Africans who, while legally entitled to be exempted from the operations of customary law under the provisions of Law 28 of 1865, still found that this exemption was a prolonged and difficult process and that even if they were exempted their children were not. The Natal Native Congress was founded at the turn of the century to broaden the appeal of political organizations beyond the mere 2000 Africans who had gained exemption certificates. Its major goals were the acquisition of the franchise on the same terms as whites and freehold land tenure.[37] According to the American Board missionary F. B. Bridgman, "They contended that these two principles were fundamental to any real solution of the racial question."[38] Bridgman was talking of a meeting between African representatives and the prime minister of Natal over the latter's proposed "reform" of legislation affecting Africans. He added, "The perfectly courteous but unwavering manner in which the natives adhered to principles they considered vital commands our admiration."[39] These two principles remained the focal point of Congress politics until the 1940s, and in some measure beyond.

The middle-class basis of the Natal Native Congress, which was later incorporated into the South African Native National Congress, was made clear in its constitution of 1915. The "objects of congress" it proclaimed, were

> to plead for and make representations for the welfare of the brown people of Natal and Zululand, and to help the Government to inquire into matters detrimental to the well-being of the brown people under the Constitution of the Union of South Africa. To assist the brown people and advise them on commercial undertakings, to seek and learn trades, including mental education and positions suitable for educated persons.
>
> The Congress shall be subject to all rules and regulations which govern all meetings of the civilised educated peoples. . . .
>
> The head offices at Pietermaritzburg shall seek work for the Natives and notify the branches of available situations[. It] will charge 1/– each person for whom it has obtained some work. . . . The Committee of Works shall find for natives and girls places where they may learn trades; shall devise ways and schemes for Natives to establish business undertakings for their benefits, and hunt for better plans to form Native Trading Companies.[40]

All this is remarkably similar to John Dube's own conception of his task at the Christian African Industrial School he established at Ohlange, and to the various schemes he engaged in to promote African business ventures, which are usually attributed to the influence of Booker T. Washington over his political and educational philosophies. Indeed as a program the constitution undoubtedly drew on the teachings of Washington, who played such an important role in spreading ideas of racial self-help and the virtues of commercial activity throughout the black diaspora. The convergence may have been the result of

Dube's personal intervention in Natal Congress Affairs or may have arisen out of the broader influences of missionary ideology in Natal, especially that of the American Board of Missions, which, through its contacts in the United States and especially with the Phelps Stokes Foundation and its director Thomas Jesse Jones, was closely in tune with developments at the more conservative black schools at Tuskegee and Hampton. For our purposes here the roots of the convergence are immaterial. What is striking is the apparent contrast between these eminently respectable and decorous Victorian Christians (one of the many African terms for the group was *Amarespectables*) — anxious to stake their claim in the burgeoning capitalist economy of South Africa, acquire freehold land, start business ventures, and lend a helping hand to employers by setting up a "Committee of Works" — and Dube's advocacy of the recognition of the Zulu monarchy at a ceremony in which 8,000 Zulu dipped their spears in "white medicine."

Dube himself melodramatically and rhetorically pointed out the contrast in his "Address to the Chiefs and People of the South African Native Congress," presented in absentia on his appointment as president in 1912:

> Upward! Into the higher places of civilization and Christianity — not backward into the slump of darkness nor downward into the abyss of the antiquated tribal system. Our salvation is not there, but in preparing ourselves for an honoured place amongst the nations.[41]

Nor is this an isolated example, although only one more quotation must suffice. In a speech in 1913 attacking government plans to segregate Africans through the Lands Act, he remarked,

> The system of tribal segregation may have suited very well a period when barbarism and darkness reigned supreme, and

nothing was required beyond those doubtful blessings, but it had the fatal defect of being essentially opposed to all enlightenment and Christianity, of utterly lacking what nowadays is our supreme requirement — the power and means of raising the native people out of the slough of ignorance, idleness, poverty [and] superstition — in a word of utter uselessness as citizens or even servants in a civilised land. The times have changed and manners must change with them.[42]

As late as 1959, the Reverend Zaccheus Mahabane, also a past president of the African National Congress (ANC) was still exhorting African Christians to overcome "ignorance, superstition, vice, degradation, barbarism, savagism, psychic unconsciousness, intellectual insensibility and mental unawareness."[43] The "acculturation" if not "deculturation" seems complete. No wonder then that Ben Magubane has roundly declared, "The supremacy of the Whites, their values and civilisation was only won when the cultural and value system of the defeated Africans was reduced to nothing, and when the Africans themselves loudly admitted the cultural hegemony of their conquerors."[44]

The reality, however, was never quite so simple. Beneath the superficial appearance of acculturation, the contrast between the mid-Victorian vision of progress and improvement on the one hand and subordination on the other led to profound tensions and ambiguities. As Phil Corrigan has reminded us, "We have to avoid reading back into history the total acceptance on the part of the apparently vanquished of the ideals and ends of their victors. . . . We should never assume a total commitment to the status quo from this appearance of acceptance."[45] In Natal-Zululand in particular, recent history, daily experience, and popular consciousness ensured a more complex reality. R. V. Selope Thema described yet another prominent member of the *kholwa* community, Pixley ka Isaka Seme, who was president of the ANC in 1930, a close colleague of Dube's, and married to Solomon's sister: "The founder was born in Natal of a Christian family. But like an African boy of the nineteenth century, he grew up in an environment which was neither African nor European: at home he was under the influence of Christian parents and American missionaries, but outside on the hills, in the valleys and the banks of the river of his beautiful country, he came into contact with the ancient life of his people and learnt about the deeds of his warrior kings."[46]

Even at the Cape, where bourgeois liberal ideology had had its triumph as a strategy of incorporating blacks into the colonial order (through, for example, the Cape's nonracial franchise and its insistence on equality before the law — though the unequal nature of the law was rarely questioned), it had little white popular support. As Stanley Trapido has remarked, Cape liberalism "depended for its legitimacy on its associations with the programmes of incorporation which the governing classes evolved in nineteenth century Britain." At the Cape, liberalism was accepted and developed because there were local structural conditions that facilitated it — essentially the interest Cape merchants, missionaries, and colonial officials had in the creation and incorporation of an independent and stable black peasantry and artisan class. Undoubtedly at the Cape, concession and incorporation were intended to defuse discontent.[47] Liberalism was meant to facilitate the creation of a nineteenth-century colonial order in which Africans would become, to quote the leading advocate of the abolition of slavery and the fostering of legitimate commerce, "some scores of millions of customers who may be taught to grow the raw material which we [i.e. the British] require and who buy the manufactured goods which we produce."[48]

Cape liberalism acted powerfully to reconcile African Christians to this order and provided them with a language of resistance when the colonial state failed to live up to the norms set by imperial ideology. This is very clear in Dube's attack on the principle of segregation in the second decade of the century and his constant appeal to "England's duty"[49] and the "white

man's burden," but it can already be heard in the language of
Tiyo Soga, one of the first black South Africans to be trained
overseas and the first Xhosa missionary, a man as outstanding in
the nineteenth century Cape as Dube was in twentieth-century
Natal. As early as the 1860s on the Cape eastern frontier, Soga
strove to reconcile his belief in the civilizing mission of empire
with his experience of its immediate rapacity.

In his recent biography of Soga, Donovan Williams has
described some of the tensions as Soga was torn between his
enthusiasm for the history and traditions of his people, and his
admiration for progress, Christianity, and "civilization," which
he identified with imperial expansion:

> Basically . . . Tiyo Soga wanted to preserve Black territorial and
> cultural integrity. British conquest was legitimate because it was a
> vehicle for civilisation ordained by God for the salvation and
> elevation of the blacks. Black society should be purged of all that
> was obnoxious to Christian morality, but not at the expense of
> intrinsic institutions and values which gave it cohesion and
> security . . . [or undermined] black dignity.[50]

Williams finds this aspect of Soga's life "fascinating, provocative
and troublesome," and explains it in terms of his "intercalary
role" as the "mediator between cultures." He argues that Soga's
nationalism and pan-Africanism (Williams goes so far as to call
Soga the father of black nationalism in South Africa) thus can be
seen "paradoxically" to have their roots in the fact that he was "a
man of two worlds."[51] Yet the dilemmas arising out of this situation were painful; the cruelties and constraints of the precolonial
African social order were not imagined, however much they may
have been matched by the ruthlessness and exploitation of colonial rule, while "civilization" brought expanded opportunities
and real advantages that could not be scorned. The very access
to print through the literacy and English language brought by
the missionaries made the new "imagined political community"
implied by nationalism a possibility.[52]

Christian Africans recognized both the meaningfulness of European "progress" and the fearful price that had to be paid. It was surely this tension that led to "the complex interplay between the poles of rejection and co-operation"[53] that characterized the politics and ideology of John Dube and the Christian African community of which he was the most outstanding representative in Natal. The interplay became even more marked in the last quarter of the nineteenth century, as mineral discoveries began to transform South Africa's political economy. Paradoxically, Kimberley, which gave educated Africans their greatest opportunity, was also the harbinger of their marginalization.

By the time the African elite was so enthusiastically improving itself, the mid-Victorian faith in the prescriptive power of "civilization" was waning. As the forces of production expanded in South Africa and made the mid-Victorian vision possible in a dramatically new way, both imperialists and Cape liberals retreated from the vision. This was not simply because, as Benedict Anderson has put it, "the expansion of the colonial state . . . invited 'natives' into schools and offices" while the expansion of "colonial capitalism . . . excluded them from boardrooms" and left them "lonely bilingual intelligentsias unattached to sturdy local bourgeoisies."[54] It was also because the demands of monopoly capital, first on the diamond fields of Kimberley, then in the gold mines of the Witwatersrand, for vast quantities of unskilled, cheap labor, and the speed with which that labor had to be conjured up, conquered, and coerced left little room in the long run for an enfranchised black peasantry and artisan class.[55] At the same time, the African elite was rendered more vulnerable by the growing insecurity that underpinned late nineteenth-century imperial expansion, and by the parallel changes in ideology increasingly shaped by social Darwinism, "Anglo-Saxon race pride," and notions of national efficiency on the one hand, together with the rise of Afrikaner nationalism and the consolidation of settler society in South Africa on the other.

In Natal, in any case, there had been little material basis for
the development of a settler liberalism from the outset, despite
the fact that its colonists were drawn almost entirely from
Victorian Britain (unlike the Cape, where about half the white
population was of Dutch or Afrikaans descent). As we have
seen, in Natal the resilience of African society and the weakness
of the colonial state (together with the unwillingness of the
British to foot the bill) had led almost from the start to a set of
policies dependent on conserving and manipulating aspects of
the African precapitalist social order. The outspoken adherence
of the ruling stratum in nineteenth-century Natal to an ideology
of segregation was by no means shared by the struggling settlers.
Indeed, the latter would have far preferred the outright
expropriation of Africans in place of the setting aside of special
reserves or locations, and the outright coercion of African labor
in place of what was termed "squatting" — the ability of
Africans to live as rent-paying tenants on Crown or other white-
owned land. At the same time their hostility to the Christian
African peasantry and landowners, some of whom were
decidedly more successful than their white counterparts, made it
far more difficult for Natal *kholwa* to model themselves on an
idealized perception of imperial middle-class society in the way
that the African intelligentsia in Kimberley with their South
African Improvement Society, the Come Again Lawn Tennis
Club, and their Eccentric Cricket Club were able to do.[56]

I do not wish to exaggerate the degree of identification of the
African intelligentsia with mid-Victorian manners even at the
Cape, nor to suggest a lack of racism there. Nevertheless, the
combination in Natal of a dominant ideology of segregation
together with virulent British settler racism, only partially
modified by a more liberal missionary ethos, made for significant differences. As early as 1860 there was an assertion of the
validity of certain African customs such as *lobola* (bridewealth)
and polygyny by black Christians in Natal, which confronted
the total condemnation of the American Board missionaries and

the colonial legal system.[57] Equally there was a recognition of the need to create links with surrounding "tribal" society.[58] And while members of the Wesleyan Methodist settlements at Driefontein and Edendale fought on the British side during the Anglo-Zulu War, and some even took up arms against the "rebels" in 1906, it is noticeable that this was not true on either occasion of converts of the American Board. Perhaps the governor of Natal in 1906, Sir Henry McCallum, was rightly suspicious of American pastors who, after all, "could not be expected to advocate the principle of honouring the King as much as that of fearing God."[59]

More significant than the suspect loyalty of American Board missionaries, however, was the increasing recognition by the turn of the century, that despite their increased education and prosperity (and the latter was by no means any longer a foregone conclusion) the *kholwa* were up against increased rather than diminished obstacles in their aspirations for acceptance as part of the colonial bourgeoisie, and in their quest for accumulation. Thus, from the late nineteenth century, the *kholwa* peasantry of Natal came under increasing pressure, as Natal's agriculture underwent dramatic transformations in response to the newly opened markets on the Rand.[60] And while some of the peasants, particularly along the line of rail, and some of the older established families were certainly able to take advantage of the new markets for a time, the increase in the white population (300 percent between 1890 and 1936),[61] the transfer of power to a white settler government in 1893, and the rise in land prices made it difficult for newcomers to compete. Drought, rinderpest (cattle disease), locusts and war all undermined the position of the peasantry in the 1890s and 1900s. Even the wealthy landowners were becoming aware that they would need to seek a larger constituency to help protect the gains they had made so far, if not to expand them. And this meant forging links with the wider African community.

It would be foolish to reduce this simply to material self-interest. For many the great crisis of commitment came with the Bambatha or Poll Tax Rebellion of 1906. In general the *kholwa* community did not participate in the uprising. Although some were swift to declare their loyalty to the colonists and condemn the "rebels,"[62] for the majority white firepower was a potent deterrent: the *kholwa* were unlikely to have shared the popular belief that if they carried out the appropriate ritual the white man's bullets would turn to water — a view prevalent among the "rebels" in Natal, as it had been in the Maji-Maji rising in German East Africa in 1905. Nor, however, did the Christian Africans respond to the Natal government's call for loyal levies with their earlier alacrity. Their incipient nationalism can be seen in the response of an American Zulu mission congregation to a white missionary's sermon based on what he had seen. It caused an uproar in his congregation, and a bitter correspondence in the columns of Dube's newspaper, *Ilange lase Natal*. Discussion with some of the leading landowners revealed that the missionary "had failed to correctly estimate the depth of feeling on the part of people who, though not in sympathy with the rebels could not hear a recital of its events from the lips of a white man without feeling that he was gloating over the success of his own race."[63] It was indeed in the year after the uprising that links between Dube and Dinuzulu, Solomon's father, were consistently forged — although there were rumours even before 1906 that Dube was in league with the ex-king and agitating for his reinstatement. With the arrest and second trial of Dinuzulu his case was taken up and reported with passion in the columns of *Ilange lase Natal*.

For the landowners of Natal and the black South African petty bourgeoisie more generally, however, the unification of white South Africa in 1910 was the first spur to more unified black action and led to the formation in 1912 of the South African Native National Congress, with John Dube as its first president. In this pan–South African political arena, the black elite saw their way forward through an inclusive, liberal-democratic nationalism. This was itself in part a challenge to the exclusive nationalism being forged by the Afrikaner petty bourgeoisie at this time, as they began to recover from the body-blows of the South African War and to mobilize against the imperial domination of South Africa's political economy. Moreover, the Union excluded African representation in the institutions of state, with the exception of the continued, qualified, non-racial franchise in the Cape. If, however, it was opposition to the Act of Union that led to the formation of the Congress, it was the 1913 Native Lands Act, to which I have already alluded, that almost immediately gave it a cause that could mobilize support far beyond the confines of its initial constituency.

The outcome of what Stanley Trapido has dubbed the "alliance of maize and gold," the 1913 Native Lands Act was designed to achieve several purposes simultaneously. Through limiting the amount of land available for African ownership to what were known as the "scheduled areas" (i.e. the existing reserves and African-owned land — some 8 percent of the total land in South Africa, increased to about 13 percent by the Native Lands and Trust Act of 1936), the Act aimed at eliminating the competition to white agriculture from African peasant production, while ensuring an exodus of workers to white-owned farms and mines, whose families could still support themselves in the rural areas (see Tables 1, 2 and 3). Outside of the scheduled areas Africans could neither purchase nor hire nor sharecrop land without the express permission of the governor-general. Thus the Act not only definitively limited the amount of land available for African purchase in the future, but it also transformed various forms of rent-paying, purchase and sharecropping arrangements into labor-tenancy and gave the landlords powerful leverage over their tenants by bringing them all under the Masters and Servants Act.[64]

Although it represented a key moment in the capitalization of South African agriculture, the Lands Act was not initially welcomed by poorer white farmers who still found accumulation

Table 1. Morgen of Land Occupied by Africans in Natal and Zululand

Class of Land	1916	1926
Rural locations (reserves)	2,897,120	3,633,210
African-owned land	176,834	131,612
Crown lands	340,802	807,133
Mission lands	152,507	146,168
White-owned lands occupied exclusively by Africans	1,012,139	290,256

Note: 1 morgen = 2,116 acres.

Table 2. Numbers of Africans on Various Classes of Land in Natal and Zululand

Class of Land	1916	1936
Reserves	479,822	693,000
Mission reserves	44,535	74,000
African-owned lands	39,250	81,000*
Crown lands	37,070	46,000
White farms	443,451	622,000
Urban areas	37,954	128,000

* Plus 10,000 on tribally purchased land.

Table 3. Total Population in Natal and Zululand

Date	White	African	Asian
Natal			
1890s	46,000 (1891)	503,208 (1894)	35,411 (1894)
Natal and Zululand			
1904	97,109	904,041	100,918
1911	98,582	951,808	141,568*
1921	136,887	1,193,804	141,600
1936	190,549	1,553,629	183,661

* In 1911 "Coloureds" (people of mixed white and African or Asian descent) were exceptionally included.

easier through rentier and sharecropping activities.[65] In Natal there was a howl of outrage from the white farmers, who alleged that their development was being threatened with "strangulation" and "asphyxiation" by the Act.[66] Not only did they object to government interference with their rentier and sharecropping activities, which had, in any case, been transformed in Natal since the 1890s by the capitalization of agriculture; more importantly they were appalled by the suggestion of the Beaumont Commission appointed under the Act that a further 3,800,000 acres (nearly one million morgen) be added to the existing 5,900,000 acres of reserve land in Zululand and Natal. The local committee appointed to revise Beaumont's findings promptly stripped this down by three quarters despite the fact that the vast bulk of land set aside for Africans was unsuited to white (and, he might have added, black) occupation, being very "malarial, sandy and badly watered."[67] The mood in white Natal was well summed up by Dr. A. W. Roberts before a Select Committee on Land in 1927: "The actual resolution taken all over Natal was that there should not be a single inch given to the natives over and above the scheduled areas."[68]

Despite their hostility to the Lands Act, white landowners were not opposed to making use of those provisions of the Act that suited their interests. While little further land was in fact acquired to relieve the congestion in the already overcrowded reserves, they were not averse to using the Act to evict those tenants who would not accept the new labor terms, or, if they preferred to maintain rent tenancies, to disguise these payments as "dipping fees" (i.e. fees demanded in exchange for dipping African-owned cattle in disinfectant against East Coast fever). By the 1920s, the Lands Act, in itself part of the process of transformation of Natal's agrarian social relations, had accelerated the growth of a considerable landless and increasingly radicalized peasantry (see below). By limiting the amount of land available for African purchase, the Lands Act seemed to the *kholwa* a mortal wound. As the Reverend Kumalo remarked before the 1917 Natal Local Native Lands Committee: "The proposed Bill will operate very harshly. . . . We have money but we are restricted from buying it [land]."[69] Chief Mbekhwe, one of the Trustees of the Methodist syndicate at Matiwane's Kop, added, "We see that the design is to deprive us of those lands we have bought with our own exertions . . . and to place us upon land upon which we cannot possibly subsist. Yet some years ago it was constantly dinned into our ears that we were lazy people who did not appreciate the advantage of buying land nor cultivating it, but now that we have awakened to its advantage we are to be restricted."[70]

The multi-faceted nature of the Act enabled the African land-owners and intelligentsia to present their class interest as the general interest, to speak on behalf of the whole African community, and with passion, although even at the time their claims did not go uncontested.[71] For Sol Plaatje, the newly appointed secretary of the South African Native National Congress, the 1913 Lands Act turned "the native into a pariah in the land of his birth."[72] Dube, who, like Plaatje, toured the countryside to record the impact of the Act, was no less scathing in his denunciation:

> The tales of misery caused to hundreds of my compatriots by the recent Native Lands Act . . . compel me to force myself on the public notice. It is only a man with a heart of stone who could hear and see what I hear and see, and yet remain callous and un-moved. It would break your hearts did you but know, as I know, the cruel and undeserved afflictions wrought by the harsh enact-ment on numberless aged, poor and tender children of this, my and their only native land. Forth from the ashes of their burnt out kraals, kicked away like dogs by Christian people from their humble hearths from the dear old scenes where their fathers were born and they grew up in simple peace, bearing malice to none and envying neither European nor Indian the wealth and plenty they can amass for themselves from this their land, these unfor-tunate outcasts pass homeless, unwanted, silently suffering along

the highways and byways of the land, seeking in vain the most unprofitable waste whereon to build their hovel and rest and live, victims of an unknown civilisation that has all too suddenly over-taken and overwhelmed them.[73]

Paradoxically, it was the 1913 Lands Act, which Dube was attacking with such vigor (and surely with an eye on the imperial humanitarian lobby whose tone he so faithfully captures), that both lent plausibility to the *kholwa* claim to speak on behalf of all Africans and undermined, then fractured, the unity of the *kholwa* community itself and led to the displacement of Dube from the presidency of Congress. For if the 1913 Lands Act unified the African opposition in the short term, in the medium term its effects were to increase the differentiation between long-established *kholwa* landowners and the evicted peasantry, who were pushed into the towns, into the reserves — and also onto the lands of black landowners. Although the amount of land privately owned by Africans actually decreased between 1916 and 1926, the number of people on it increased from 39,000 to 81,000.[74]

While the small number of more successful African farmers (an increasing number of whom began sugar cultivation in the mid-1920s)[75] allowed labor-tenants onto their land, those less able to compete with capitalist agriculture, because of lack of credit and technology and poorer access to the market, turned to landlordism. Increasingly, the *kholwa* landowners became rentiers, allowing the evicted to settle on their lands in exchange for a money-rent, now earned not through petty commodity production but through wage-labor in the towns and mines. As a result, the interwar years saw the acceleration of a process that changed the once flourishing mission settlements and syndicate lands into rural slums. By 1933 the Wesleyan Methodist settlement at Edendale, which we described in its mid – nineteenth-century heyday with 450 inhabitants, now had 5,000. In 1938 the Thornton Committee on Health described Edendale in terms very different from those of the glowing travellers' reports of the nineteenth century:

> The sanitary conditions at Edendale were deplorable in the extreme. . . . The dwellings consist for the most part of ill-lit and very badly ventilated wattle and daub structures, often without sanitary conveniences. When the latter are provided, they are mostly insanitary and badly sited. It is, therefore, not surprising that epidemics have occurred at Edendale in the past and conditions are such that further outbreaks are expected at any time.[76]

Edendale, which acted increasingly as a commuter suburb for the city of Pietermaritzburg, was perhaps hit particularly hard; nevertheless a widespread picture of faction-ridden, impoverished, and divided communities emerges from the state and mission records of the interwar years, with serious tensions between landlords and their tenants, and landlords and the rural landless. As one Mpofu Ogle remarked before the 1917 Local Lands Committee, Africans who have bought land "are hated by those who have no land. . . . There are a large number of natives who are without fields owing to the greed of others in demanding a larger amount of land than they are entitled to."[77]

Dube himself put the point equally clearly before a missionary conference in Johannesburg in 1925, when he remarked that "the prosperity of the native Christians rouses jealousy among the other members of the tribe and the chief himself. A cry is raised that the Kholwas are using up all the land . . . [and] cattle have nowhere to graze."[78] Initially, through Dube's activities and those of the South African Native National Congress, it seemed as though these contradictions could be contained. In 1917, however, Dube was ousted from the presidency of the national organization, ostensibly because of his acquiescence in "the principle of segregation so far as it can be fairly and practically carried out,"[79] but in fact probably because by then part of the national organization, especially on the Rand, was becoming rather more radical than its Natal leader.[80] Be that as it may, it is in Dube's need to look once again for a more local constituency, at a time of increased state emphasis on the ideology of segregation and of rising tension within African society in Natal, that part of the answer to our conundrum of his funeral oration may be sought.

Dube severed his ties with the SANNC's national executive in 1917 as the result of his being ousted from the national presidency. Over the next thirty years the Congress movement in Natal was bedeviled by factions, with an official branch still adhering to the national organization and a more conservative Natal Native Congress, which was dominated by Dube and probably represented the larger landowners. It was only after the death of Dube in 1946 that George Champion, through adroit political maneuvering, brought the two Natal organizations together again and more fully into the orbit of the national organization. Tensions remained, indeed, until the election of Albert Luthuli, first as president of the provincial Congress and then as national president.[81]

After 1917, forced to mobilize his own constituency, Dube seems to have turned increasingly to the Zulu royal family, and to the rich history and ritual it provided for ethnic nationalism. The recent memories of conquest and the dramatic quality of the Zulu past and royal symbolism provided a ready source of material for an indigenous "refurbishing of traditionalism," which was reinforced by the state's efforts in the same direction. At the same time, Dube continued to believe in progress through education and accumulation, and to preach the virtues of thrift and industry. A founder in the early thirties of the Bantu Business League (one of many similar organizations designed to assist small African businessmen), Dube was clearly engaged in a number of entrepreneurial schemes as well as in sugar-planting.[82] This may have lain behind George Champion's description of his old enemy in 1937: "Mr Dube is a business man and a politician. His capitalistic views do not agree with those of the masses."[83] The characterization was not so much unfair as somewhat hypocritical, given Champion's almost identical class position; his rhetoric, as we shall see, was much more populist. Both Dube and Champion, however, had to find a larger constituency; both turned to the Zulu royal family as part of the strategy for doing so.

As Tom Nairn has put it in an important article on nationalism entitled "The Modern Janus," elites on the periphery have "had to contest the concrete form in which . . . progress had taken them by the throat, even as they set out to progress by themselves."[84] To defend and expand their opportunities they had in turn to mobilize their own society and consciously create a "militant inter-class community rendered strongly (if mystically) aware of its own separate identity vis-à-vis the outside forces of domination":

> Mobilisation had to be in terms of what was there; and the whole point of the dilemma was that there was nothing there. . . . All that there *was* was the people and the peculiarities of the region: its inherited *ethos*, speech, folklore, and so on. Nationalism works through differentiae like those because it has to. It is not necessarily democratic in outlook, but it *is* invariably populist.[85]

In the South African case this mobilization was rendered difficult because of the double defense that had to be mounted — against metropolitan imperialism and the more immediate threat of settler encroachment. Moreover, the most virulently hostile of the settlers had seized these very weapons for their own defense against the imperialist thrust in their creation of Afrikaner nationalism. An appeal to imperial and nineteenth-century liberal norms was the logical response for those who had witnessed the rapacity of colonial encroachment on African lands, the ferocity with which Afrikaner commandoes threatened to end the franchise of the black communities during the Anglo-Boer War, or the savagery with which Natal had put down the Bambatha Rebellion.

The problem was that this language of resistance could hardly mobilize a mass movement — especially by the 1920s when the many appeals by the nationalist elite for imperial intervention had manifestly failed to deliver the goods. The result was a discourse in which Dube appealed to several different audiences simultaneously. On the whole, American scholars have heard the voice of Booker T. Washington, British liberals that of Victorian liberalism.[86] The Zulu ethnic nationalism directed at his home constituency has been relatively unexplored by historians, but was a crucial part of Dube's rhetoric. And as the state itself came to support its variant of ethnicity in terms of Hertzog's segregationist policies,[87] this gave Dube and his confreres further impetus and leverage.

The links between Dube and the Zulu royal family were of course not initiated simply in response to the increasing segregationalism of the state. As we have seen he had already been roused by the fate of Dinuzulu after the Bambatha Rebellion. Present at Dinuzulu's funeral, Dube had acted informally as an adviser to the young Solomon in the years that followed. Nevertheless, it was only after 1918 or 1919 that those looser connections began to take political shape, in the meetings between the members of the Zulu royal family and their immediate circle and the Natal *kholwa*, who were largely led by Dube. Thus, according to the missionary L. H. Oscroft, the Zulu National Council or *Inkatha* (precursor of the National Cultural Liberation Movement founded in 1975 by Chief Gatsha Buthelezi) owed its origins in 1922 – 1923 to both the deliberate resuscitation by the Zulu royal family of traditional forms and the active collaboration in the process of "educated natives from outside."[88] The first *Inkatha* was closely associated with the raising of a Zulu National Fund, which was alleged to have £3,000 banked in Vryheid in 1923 and was used to pay off debts of the Zulu royal family (which were considerable); the intention was also to use the funds "for the benefit of the Zulu nation from time to time."[89]

At a 500-strong meeting of *Inkatha* in 1924 the matters discussed included the building of a national church, which the royal family wished to be called the "Chaka Zulu's Church" (though *kholwa* opposition led to a change in name to the Zulu National Church); the Zulu National Fund, the resolution of divisions within the Zulu royal family, which went back to Cetshwayo's day; and opposition to the introduction of the council system on the Transkei model into Zululand because the meeting maintained that "the present means of government through Solomon and the chiefs should not be interfered with."[90] According to Oscroft once again, "the real object" of *Inkatha* was "to unite all black races . . . they consider that the native is victimised in many ways and receives unfair and unjust treatment from the white man; that this will continue as long as the natives are divided; that the native people will never be strong until there is unity among them. They are casting around for a rallying point — a central figure — and that figure would seem to be Solomon."[91]

For the *kholwa* landowners and petty bourgeoisie the royal family could perform functions that the subordinate chiefs recognized by the Natal administration could not (despite the linkages between the chiefs and the royal family). The royal family could play a role in pan-Zulu nationalism and also a self-consciously modernizing role. The position of the king was likened to that of the king of England as a constitutional monarch — perhaps not surprisingly given *kholwa* ideological formation and the enormous strength in nineteenth-century South Africa of the myth of "The Great White Queen" as the symbol of imperial hegemony. Nor should one forget the powerful missionary symbolism of "Christ the King." By 1928 Wheelwright, the chief native commissioner, could remark with alarm on the extent to which African political organizations were courting Solomon's favor, notwithstanding the fact that "the emergence of strong democratic political bodies among the Native people would tend to undermine the comparative autonomy of the Chiefs which he represents." To Wheelwright's dismay, business letters, political circulars, and postcards were all being circulated with Solomon's photograph inscribed "King of the Zulu."[92]

Solomon was not slow to encourage their belief that he could become a model constitutional monarch, as he advocated increased educational and industrial opportunities for his people, while pleading for the continuance of the "Zulu tribal system," and extolling "the traditional merits of his race, the virtue of our women and the honesty of our people."[93] The 1932 Native Economic Commission elicited a surprising degree of support among the educated elite for the Zulu paramountcy and the tribal system, even if this was hedged about somewhat. Thus within the specifically Natal-Zululand political arena, the elements of popular consciousness associated with the monarchy were now being woven into a new, essentially conservative ideology in which the king became "the pivot of Zulu cultural life."[94] This was most explicit in the foundation in 1935 of the Zulu Society by the Natal Bantu Teachers' Association, for the promotion of "Zulu cultural identity." It had as one of its chief roles lobbying the government to recognize the Zulu para-mountcy.[95] It should come as no surprise that John Dube was first president and that the regent, Mshiyeni, who followed Solomon, was its honorary patron.

Nor were these ideological roles the only ones the Zulu royal family could play. Above all, it can be argued that with the sharpening of class conflict in Natal and also in the Zulu country-side in the 1920s and the rise of the Industrial and Commercial Workers' Union (ICU), which we discuss in the next chapter, the Zulu royal family and the traditionalism it represented con-stituted a bulwark against radical change, as much for the wealthier African landowners and the chiefs as for the ideo-logues of segregation. This indeed was recognized by Solomon in a bitter attack on Champion and the ICU in August 1927. Commenting in *Ilanga lase Natal*, Dube took the opportunity of the English translation to make his message even more explicit:

> The organisation would be a good thing in industrial centres if the
> ideal aimed at was the amelioration of conditions under which
> Natives labour, and to secure those means by co-operation of
> both Natives and Europeans. But he [Solomon] regards the
> leaders as very dangerous. . . . The ICU are exploiting poor
> Native workers. . . . The leaders are irresponsible, they do not
> understand the relation of capital to labour, the need for invest-
> ment. . . . What workers are they looking for in the native areas
> and reserves? Are any of the leaders engaged in business employ-
> ing a number of people for farming and paying 8 shillings a day
> for their workers? How about that for men of Groutville, Aman-
> zimtoti and Ifafa! Are they prepared to pay their employee that
> wage? How long can they raise cane at a profit if they pay such
> wages?[96]

By 1930, there is evidence that Solomon's hostility to the ICU
had considerably abated, and he and Champion appear to have
established a cordial relationship, though it was masked on
Solomon's side by his usual deference to the officials who looked
with dismay on the accord.[97] That twist to the story must be
explored in the next chapter, however. Here I would like to end
with a reflection on the following remarks by John Foster in his
Class Struggle and the Industrial Revolution:

> The patterns of culture that define any group's identity are not
> arbitrary but concrete, based upon historically determined levels
> of consumption. And the job of maintaining and defending this
> identity is clearly integral to the structure of any particular
> grouping. It cannot be imposed from outside. To maintain itself
> in a technologically changing society, a sub-group has to accept
> and reject. And within most it is possible to identify two distinct
> groupings (or "poles") of leaders, one trying to open it up to
> developments in society at large (and especially to the rapidly
> changing occupational and cultural demands put upon it); the
> other — mediating at a more intense level — defending its

traditional identity and particularly the objective rights and standards used to define it against others.[98]

Foster is of course writing about early nineteenth-century England, where the "poles" did perhaps remain apart. In the periphery, as Nairn suggests, acceptance and rejection go hand in hand. For Dube, and for others like him, the central ambiguity of nationalism was rendered even more equivocal by his need to simultaneously espouse nineteenth-century liberal and missionary norms against settler nationalism on the one hand, and to call on the masses while defending his own position against the masses on the other. Some of these ambiguities are neatly encapsulated in the invitation extended by John Dube to the governor-general (still widely regarded as the representative of imperial rather than settler hegemony) to unveil a monument at Stanger to commemorate Shaka, "who is looked upon as the founder of the Zulu nation and power."[99]

CHAPTER 3

George Champion
and the Ambiguities of Class
and Class Consciousness

This chapter starts with a rather longer tale of ambiguity and paradox. In September 1930 Allison Wessels George Champion, leader of the Industrial and Commercial Workers' Union of Natal (known as the ICU Yase Natal) received a notice from the minister of justice banning him from most of Natal under the newly amended Riotous Assemblies Act. Champion, who was described by Margery Perham in 1929 as "the arch agitator of the Union,"[1] (whether of South Africa or the workers is not clear), had been a thorn in the flesh of the local authorities from the moment of his arrival in Durban as the secretary of the ICU in 1925.

The ICU had been founded by a Malawian, Clements Kadalie, among dockworkers in Cape Town in 1919; by the mid-1920s it had developed into a mass protest movement throughout southern Africa. An "all-in" union, it drew its adherents both from the intelligentsia and the newly proletarianized in the towns and from the dispossessed squatters and peasants in the countryside.[2] Although the organization was initially slow to get off the ground in Natal, within eighteen months of his arrival, Champion had built up an organization with fifty-eight secretaries, clerks and organizers.[3] To quote Chief Justice de Waal, Champion was "in many respects a remarkable man. Of good Zulu parentage, well educated, in the prime of life, held in high esteem by and exercising great influence over his fellows, he is capable of much good and infinite

8. *A.W.G. Champion as a young man outside the ICU headquarters in Johannesburg, early 1920s* (UNISA Africana collection).

9. *A.W.G. Champion in his old age in the 1970s* (UNISA Africana collection).

10. Rioting by whites outside the headquarters of the ICU in Prince Edward Street, Durban, during the 1929 "beerhall riots" (*Natal Mercury*, 19.6.1929, Killie Campbell Library).

11. Crowd scene in Victoria Street, Durban, during the 1929 "beerhall riots" (Local History Museum, Durban).

12. Member of the South African Police examining poll-tax receipts and defaulters awaiting removal to jail, Durban, 1929 (Local History Museum, Durban).

mischief. . . . his arrival caused a change to come over the scene."[4]

By 1925 Champion already had considerable experience in causing what Chief Justice de Waal was pleased to call "infinite mischief." The son of a convert of the American Board of Missions, he was educated for a time at the famous Amanzimtoti Institute (later Adams College), the American Congregationalist school not far from Durban, before entering the police force. After a spell on the Rand, he served as a special constable in Dundee and Babanango, part of his duties being to spy on the Zulu royal family. His mother, Nomazembe Cele, persuaded him, however, "to leave the Police and get other employment . . . because my father had been a soldier in the army when the British troops fought against the Zulus. 'Why should you again follow in the steps of your father against your own people?'" she asked.[5] Champion now went to the Rand to work at the mines. By 1920 he was employed at Crown Mines as a clerk and within a short while headed the Transvaal Native Clerks' Association, agitating for higher wages and "disputing the welfare of the workers,"[6] as well as giving evidence before several government commissions. In Johannesburg he was a member of the newly formed Joint Council of Europeans and Natives and became part of its executive committee.

In 1925, when the headquarters of the ICU was moved from Cape Town to Johannesburg, Champion was persuaded by Kadalie to leave Crown Mines and become organizing secretary for the Transvaal; a few months later he was sent to Durban to organize the fledgling movement. Here, he rose rapidly to the forefront as a leader, both in Natal and nationally, taking Kadalie's place as national organizing secretary when the latter was abroad. As Chief Justice de Waal acknowledged, in Natal his activities transformed the position of the organization. By 1927 there were said to be over 50,000 members of the ICU in the province; 26,000 of them were in Durban alone — a remarkable number if correct, for there were only between

35,000 and 40,000 Africans officially in the town.[7] Funds from the province had become the mainstay of the head office in Johannesburg. In 1928, after financial scandals implicating ICU officers in Natal had erupted in the local courts and Champion's own honesty and judgement had been under suspicion, he was suspended from the national organization; such was his standing, however, that he was able to take most of the local organization and membership of the ICU with him into the independent ICU Yase Natal. As A. F. Batty, the one-time British trade-unionist and veteran socialist, who had encouraged Kadalie to initiate the ICU in Cape Town in 1919 and later became Champion's friend and counsellor, wrote when the latter was suspended, "thousands of natives in this town . . . rose in might against the victimization . . . of their leader" and insisted on his reinstatement.[8]

Champion's popularity was largely the result of the notable series of legal battles he had won in close association with a white lawyer, Cecil Cowley, against both the Durban Corporation and local employers in the previous years. Among his most important successes were the abolition of the nightly curfew for black residents and the removal from the pass (the document every African had — and has — to carry in order to prove his right to be in an urban area) of the so-called character column, where an unfavorable comment by an employer could well jeopardize further employment. He also accomplished the exempting of black women from carrying night passes; the lifting of prohibitions on Africans renting rooms and engaging in trade in the town; the restraining of the police from summarily demanding passes; and the ending of the system whereby Africans could be tried in batches for the same offenses, with policemen acting as interpreters. In addition one of his most notable victories was the abolition of what was known as "the bodily dipping of natives," the compulsory disinfecting of blacks on their entry into the city as an antityphus measure.[9] A series of letters to employers about wrongful dismissal and threatening legal action unless workers were given pay in lieu of notice had not enhanced his popularity with the white citizens of Durban.[10] As Maynard Swanson has pointed out, "these manoeuvres were of course at best tactical and short-run victories. . . . In their context, however, and in their manner of achievement they represented unprecedented concessions wrung from a rather surprised and increasingly indignant white community. They provided the visibility for Champion and the gratification for his public from which he acquired great influence for himself and his union."[11] His legal victories, while undoubtedly discomforting to the Durban Corporation, served to confirm the social order rather than invalidate it. But while they certainly did not challenge the social order's "rampant inequalities," they clearly increased Champion's standing in the black community.

It was his instigation of a boycott to challenge the municipal monopoly of beerbrewing, however, that gave Champion the opportunity of mass support, both in Durban and in the smaller towns of Natal. This was particularly important because by 1929 the popularity of the ICU may well have already peaked as evidence of financial mismanagement and the disagreements between Kadalie and Champion began to affect morale throughout the organization. In opposing the extension of the so-called Durban system, whereby municipal revenues were raised through the sale of what was inelegantly known as "kaffir beer" (i.e. *utshwala*, the traditional beer that was an integral part of African diet), Champion had fastened on an issue that roused widespread popular resistance.

Although the mining houses on the Witwatersrand had early recognized the potential of alcohol as an instrument of social control in the compounds, it is to the Corporation of Durban that the dubious honor belongs of having pioneered the municipal monopoly of the manufacture and distribution of *utshwala* in order to finance African welfare. This tidy expedient got the poorest members of the community to pay both for their own services and for one of the instruments of their subordination.[12] Under Act 23 of 1908, Durban had been able to raise no less that £283,627 in 20 years and had used it to build a brewery, barracks, and eating houses for workers as well as a hospital and a couple of schools.[13] By the 1920s, the Durban system was widely admired as a method of raising revenue and of keeping down drunkenness, since the alcohol content of municipal beer could be so much more easily controlled than if it were left to the discretion of African brewers. Thus the 1923 Native Urban Areas Act, which replaced Natal's "Native Beer Act," encouraged municipalities in the rest of South Africa to copy the Natal example and establish municipal beer monopolies for Africans. Under the 1923 Act, African women were prohibited from entering the beerhalls.

It was the spread of the Durban system to the smaller towns and municipalities of Natal, and its extension beyond municipal boundaries through the 1928 Liquor Act, that enabled Champion to mobilize support. Oppressive as the earlier legislation had been, African women had been able to sidestep some of its restrictions by brewing beer for domestic consumption. Many had been able to smuggle the beer into the towns or to sell it on or just beyond the municipal boundaries. Under the new legislation, these evasions were no longer possible. At the same time, the new Act also made it necessary for Africans on farms to have the permission of both the local magistrate and the European landowner before they could brew, while even the possession of *utshwala* became illegal in the reserves.[14] The chief native commissioner of Natal was forced to admit that the effect of the new act "undoubtedly presses very hard on the people."[15]

The first rumblings of protest began to be heard in May 1929 when the local Administration and Health Board of Sydenham (then beyond the municipal boundaries of Durban) published its intentions of applying for a monopoly of beer halls in terms of section 21(1) of the Native Urban Areas Act. On 3 May Champion addressed the board on behalf of the ICU: "Our

Union does not favour the manufacture and sale of kaffir beer by Health Boards or Municipalities. They protest against any attempt to obtain money from the poor natives by selling to them intoxicating liquor brewed by the local Governments and they feel that such means of obtaining money from the natives is not a proper and honest way of maintaining the Western civilisation in this land."[16] A further letter of protest was followed and reinforced by two organized marches from the ICU hall in Durban to Sydenham, headed at least on the first occasion "by a brass band, a native in . . . a kilt . . . a Union Jack and a red flag with a hammer and sickle on it."[17] The marches passed off with little more than a couple of minor skirmishes with local passers-by.[18]

In mid-June, however, matters took a turn for the worse, when the heavy-handed actions of the compound manager at one of the barracks at the Point in Durban's harbor area, led to the declaration of a boycott of the beer halls by the dockworkers, the most militant and organized element in the Durban workforce.[19] The dockworkers' cause was taken up by the ICU, and at a meeting on the sand dunes opposite their barracks Champion openly advocated a boycott of the beer halls. When, on 17 June, in an attempt to enforce their boycott, the dockworkers clashed with the police, serious trouble appeared imminent. Champion was called in and was driven to the scene by the police. At the barracks, Champion, according to both his own account and that of Captain Baston of the South African police, offered "whatever assistance he could for the preservation of law and order" and was able to calm the "somewhat unruly" crowd. The men were persuaded to disperse.[20] Before this was known, however, an angry white mob had surrounded the ICU headquarters, and in the ensuing melee seven people were killed (two whites and five blacks) and eighty-four injured. That day and the next, white civilians besieged the ICU hall and set to work wrecking ICU property.

From Sydenham and Durban, the unrest spread to Pinetown,

Howick, Ladysmith, Weenen, and the Glencoe coal mines.[21]
Here the demonstrators were generally African women, many of
them already suffering from the famine that was to afflict Natal
for the next three years. As one of a group of some 500 women
told the magistrate of Dundee in September 1929, "We are starv-
ing and we wear sacks because our husbands spend their money
and time at the Beer Halls. . . . This beer is our old food; the
food of our forefathers. When we make beer for ourselves the
Sergeant raids homes." Another added,

> We appeal to the government — we never have any rest. When we
> make our tea [i.e. African beer] the police are always raiding us.
> Our floors are dug up and every day we have to put new floors
> down. When we make beer for our husbands we take it to where
> they are working and on their return they find no-one at the kraal
> for we have been arrested. The Government does not protect us.
> Our husbands spend all their money at the beerhalls and do not
> give us any.[22]

It was not simply, as the chief native commissioner thought,
that the women wanted access to beer for their own consumption,[23] or even — as was undoubtedly partly true — that "the
beer monopoly made inroads on the lucrative *shebeen* (illicit
liquor) trade, thereby destroying one of the few fields open to
African enterprise."[24] Male expenditure in the beer hall was
doubly crippling for the household; not only was much-needed
cash being spent, but the new legislation also undercut what had
hitherto been an important way in which women could subsidize
family income. In the smaller towns and in the peripheral areas
around Durban, where there was still access to land and grain,
women frequently brewed for sale as well as home consumption.
Now money that had hitherto been redistributed within and
between households went into municipal coffers or, at the
mines, into the trader's store.[25] The response of the women in
the small towns closely resembles that of the eighteenth-century
food rioters described by E. P. Thompson as they sought the

restoration of a lost right and appealed to the government for justice.

Antagonism over the beer monopoly added to the many other issues causing dissatisfaction and disaffection in the countryside. Inspectors responsible for checking the dipping of African stock were met with hostility and obstruction. One group of women told the officials at the dipping tank in Bergville, "During the Great War the Europeans took our men and children and drowned them, now they want to drown our goats." In other areas, too, women resisted the demands of the police and local authorities, perhaps encouraged by their peers.[26] Champion was swiftly on the scene, and the women were organized into an auxiliary branch of the ICU Yase Natal. Yet the struggle was not a success — according to Champion "because only women took an active part. . . . their men were in collusion with the Government and Local Authorities."[27] As at other times and in other places, the men felt threatened by the militancy of their wives and resented the absence of creature comforts that their wives' political activities entailed.

The riot in Durban was followed by a government commission, which had some harsh things to say about Champion,[28] and a visit to Durban by the government-appointed advisory Native Affairs Commission in December 1929. The commission reported "with some reluctance" that Champion had "established an influence which . . . is . . . fraught with dangerous consequences."[29] It reminded the minister for Native Affairs that, under the recently passed Riotous Assemblies Act, "the Governor-General has, as Supreme Chief, the power to remove a Native to parts where his activities may be curtailed and, while not recommending that this power be exercised in respect of Champion, the Commission feels that it may be necessary in the future, unless the situation changes in Durban."[30] The minister waited another nine months before using these powers.

The delay is noteworthy.[31] The new 1929 Nationalist government under J.B.M. Hertzog elected on a "black-peril" platform, could hardly be accused in general of adopting a kid-glove approach to "native agitators." It was obsessed at this time not only with the ICU, but with the increased activities of the communists and the radicalization of the African National Congress. The spread among blacks of Garveyite ideas from the United States and the evident hostility to whites expressed in the slogan, "Africa for the Africans," added to the ferment in town and countryside and increased the disquiet in ruling-class circles.[32] It was to combat all these activities, indeed, that the Riotous Assemblies (Amendment) Act (no.19) of 1929, under whose terms Champion was eventually banished, was passed. As a reassertion of state control in November 1929, the minister of justice, Oswald Pirow, deemed it necessary himself to lead a raid at three o'clock in the morning of 500 mounted police from the Transvaal on the Durban barracks and compounds, demanding passes and tax receipts and confiscating potential weapons. As the *Star* newspaper laconically reported, "when the natives saw the machine guns and bayonets, they acquiesced readily to the police search for Poll Tax defaulters." Just to make sure, three tear-gas bombs were also lobbed into the men leaving the compounds for work, and "the effectiveness of the new police arm for mass control was immediately demonstrated."[33] Over 500 Africans were arrested on various charges.

Nevertheless, the beer boycott continued through most of 1929. As Champion wrote shortly after this raid to his friend and sympathizer, Sibusisiwe (Violet) Makhanya, "Durban is dry, no kaffir beer is drunk by natives."[34] The City Fathers, perturbed by the potential loss of some sixty thousand pounds in annual revenue and disturbed by the depth of African discontent, decided to match — if somewhat unequally — coercion with reform. As elsewhere and at other times in South Africa (notably during World War II, and after 1976), reform was part of the ruling class response to social unrest and was closely related to a preceding period of popular militancy.[35] In August 1929 the Rotary Club urged the Durban City Council to develop "Native Recreation on an organized basis" and offered financial assistance both for this and for the appointment of a "Native Welfare Officer."[36] A similar resolution was passed by the Natal Missionary Council. At the beginning of 1930, the City Council established a Native Administration Committee to deal exclusively with matters relating to Africans and appointed a Native Advisory Board consisting of four city councillors and ten Africans drawn as representatives from Durban's political and church organizations as well as the barracks. At the same time, the council appointed a welfare officer "charged with the responsibility of investigating complaints, grievances, and organising social entertainments, sports and recreation."[37] Sports and recreation now became a key part of the strategy for diffusing discontent.[38] According to the *Mayor's Minute* in the city's annual report:

> The Corporation . . . continued its policy of providing free bioscope entertainments at the various Native Barracks and Institutions including the Native Women's Hostel in Grey Street. . . . At the various barracks and locations, indoor games — draughts, ping-pong and the like — are provided by the council for the enjoyment of the Natives; a tennis court is in use and others are under construction, and more will be provided if it be found that there is a demand for them. Several football grounds are in use . . . but the increasing demand makes the provision of further grounds desirable, and no doubt these will be provided in the near future.[39]

The mayor proposed to form a "Native Bugle Band,"[40] perhaps inspired by the drums and pipes on the ICU march! This strategy of what the missionary, Ray Phillips, called "moralizing leisure time"[41] had long been advocated by missionaries of the American Board and drew on familiar precedents from the United States, where, according to a local newspaper "the expenditure on such facilities [had] saved several times over . . . the expenditure on the police force. . . . Recreation . . . was the railing at the top of the precipice that saved the necessity for a hospital and a cemetery at the bottom."[42]

Durban now explicitly modeled its response on that of Johannesburg, where African working-class militancy after World War I had made some form of liberalization crucial; there, too, the transatlantic connection had been uppermost in reformers' minds. The City Council in Durban purchased 3,000 acres of land to establish a segregated "Native village on thoroughly progressive and up-to-date lines" and bathing booths and lavatory accommodation was provided "on that portion of the Beach now set aside for the use of the Native People." Unfortunately "that portion of the Beach" was "on a somewhat dangerous" part of the coast, but the mayor thought this disadvantage could be overcome easily by encouraging a native life-saving corps.[43] More seriously, the first steps were taken to construct a new African urban location at Umlazi, on mission land beyond the borough boundary.[44] Finally, it was hoped that the appointment of the South Africa – wide Native Economic Commission would lead to an improvement in "native affairs" through its investigation of conditions of employment, wage rates, legislation affecting workers, and the proportion of revenue Africans contributed directly and indirectly to the public purse.

The mayor concluded his summary of the activities of the council on a note of self-congratulation. He thought they provided "an interesting reply to the unrest and agitation displayed by Natives in recent years" and felt that the year had "marked a definite advance in the Corporation's management of its Native Affairs and considerable progress [had] been made in meeting the legitimate requests and requirements of the Zulu population in Durban."[45]

Champion, too, professed himself well satisfied, offered the full collaboration of the ICU with the Native Advisory Board and Welfare Officer, and claimed a large share of the credit for these achievements.[46] He became a member of the first Native Advisory Board, one of the two representatives granted to the

ICU yase Natal, and showed every intention of working perfectly happily within the newly established system. In August 1930 he was apparently even planning retirement from the union because he "had promised Mr. Justice de Waal that if the Durban Town Council would establish the Native Advisory Board I would retire." More importantly, he had decided, "I wanted to teach my Native people Commerce."[47] So satisfactory was his conduct that when the mayor of Durban heard that the government had served a banning order on Champion he was appalled. As he wrote to the minister of justice on 26 September:

> For the last year relations between Whites and Blacks have been improving in Durban and throughout Natal (and all have hailed with relief the appointment of the Economic Commission which we feel will do more to place matters on a permanent good footing than could any other agency . . .). I have been approached by many men of good will . . . who think with me that we should ask you to suspend the order issued against Champion for so long as he observes his present solemn engagement to take no further part in public affairs. Those of us who know him best believe that he is entirely sincere in his promises and that he will keep them. As a matter of policy, too, I feel that it would be very unwise to make Champion into a martyr. . . . If you accept Champion's promises you have disposed of him not less effectively than were he deported: you would have had the last word: and then Champion's influence would be more completely destroyed than were he removed to any other part of South Africa.[48]

The mayor was overly sanguine about the municipality's co-optive strategy. The Communist party had benefited greatly from the decline in the ICU, which predated Champion's departure and was related to the financial problems of the organization and its internal dissensions.[49] When the party called on workers to burn their hated passes on 16 December, Durban, of all cities, and the dockworkers at the Point, of all workers, responded with an enthusiasm noticeably absent elsewhere.

Inspired by the leadership of a young communist, Johannes Nkosi, a huge crowd assembled at Cartwright Flats, undeterred by the rival attempts of the now ultracautious leadership of the ICU Yase Natal to prevent any action.[50] After four hours of speeches, the crowd began a march in demonstration on Durban, and the police barred their way. The procession was attacked with ferocity and Nkosi and three others were stabbed to death.

After this further defeat, Durban slowly simmered down. The forcible removal of several thousand unemployed workers from Durban back to the rural areas as the effects of the world depression began to take effect was probably as important as the display of force and certainly more important than Champion's disappearance from the scene.[51] By March 1931 Detective Inspector Arnold of the Criminal Investigation Department in Durban could remark with satisfaction that, as a result of the action taken on 16 December and the prosecution of the participants, "the general situation here has developed into all the various organizations falling apart and practically losing all membership and former power, mistrust having generally taken root amongst the Native population."[52] Detective Inspector Arnold could take particular credit for the outcome: as a close confidant of Champion, he had been largely instrumental — with A. F. Batty — in urging Champion to split from the national ICU at the time of his suspension in 1929, and in drawing up a new constitution for the ICU yase Natal. Thus, according to Champion in his evidence to the Durban Riots Commission,

> Mr Arnold has been our friend all along, and he has attended our committee meetings and taken part in the framing of our constitution. I knew him as a detective when I was a Policeman myself. In fact he was a member of the ICU. Our constitution was actually typewritten through his courtesy in his own office. . . . He knows me and where I live and attended me during my sickness and bought medicine for me at his own expense. . . . I knew that Sergeant Arnold was a detective and on duty when he attended

our meetings, but I was afraid of nothing as I had nothing to hide.[53]

In exile in Johannesburg, ironically, Champion was found a job in the Colonial Banking and Trust Company through the good offices of the director of native labour, Major H. S. Cooke. His banning order was finally lifted at the end of 1934 — after the death of Solomon ka Dinuzulu. This may, of course, have been coincidence. There can, however, be no doubt that the immediate precipitant for his banning order was not, as has generally been assumed, the beer hall riots, but Champion's meeting with Solomon in Durban at the end of August and beginning of September 1930.[54] Champion himself acknowledged this in an unpublished memoir written towards the end of his life: "It was in 1930 after I had been visited by the King of the Zulus . . . Solomon ka Dinuzulu, that I was ordered to leave Durban for twelve months from 24th September. The period was extended for two years more, because I had refused to accept terms."[55]

Solomon's account of the affair was typically evasive. Charged with having had dealings with the ICU by the chief native commissioner he indignantly retaliated by calling the allegation "just lies." He maintained that he had been recognized quite by chance on the evening of 31 August when he had almost fortuitously entered the ICU Social Centre:

> Then Champion extended a public welcome to me. He said he was very pleased to see me because they [the ICU] were despised, even by Dube. . . . I made no reply, but later I sent for Champion in his office and asked him why he made enemies with the white people, why did he talk dirty? I told him I had just come to look, but was not pleased with the words he had spoken. I said last year in Durban people were killed. Where was he when they were killed? It was the words he had spoken that had killed those people. . . . I concluded by saying that if the rule was still a black

rule he would be killed for what he had done. He asked me if I
would go . . . to a meeting the following Saturday. I said I would
think it over. He issued notices to say I would be there. I thought
it over and decided to stay away as things may be done which I
may not approve of.[56]

Despite his earlier denunciations of Champion, this was
Solomon once again donning his mask of deference before the
chief native commissioner. As private letters at the time,
Solomon's subsequent behavior, and Champion's continued,
though at times troubled, liaison with the Zulu royal family
through the thirties and forties make clear, the Durban meetings
had indeed effected a reconciliation between the king and the
man he had been happy to dub "irresponsible," "dangerous,"
and an exploiter of "poor Native workers" only three years
before.[57]

   Once again this story presents us with many puzzles — to start
with, the state's actions. Here, as we have already noted, what is
surprising is that the authorities waited so long before removing
Champion from the scene. Manifestly, the meetings with
Solomon were the final precipitant for a course of action that
had many earlier justifications. As we have seen, it was through
the Zulu royal family that the state hoped to "refurbish traditionalism" and to strengthen its hold over the chiefs and its rural
network of control — even if that refurbishing had to stop short
of recognizing Solomon's paramountcy. The thought that
Champion himself might use the same network and perhaps
radicalize it was clearly disconcerting.

   Early in 1930 Champion had held a meeting of Natal and
Zululand chiefs. In an effort to counter any notion that the ICU
was opposed to the chieftaincy, Champion assured those
assembled that his purpose was simply to secure "their goodwill
and co-operation" and bring them together "in order that they
might know what their children were suffering."[58] As Commissioner of Police I. P. de Villiers saw it:

> There is no doubt whatever that Champion, with the assistance of Solomon, has gained a very considerable footing amongst the Zulu chiefs and that coincident with this the meetings of the ICU have become inflammatory in nature. There is also no doubt whatever that Champion, by reason of his association with Solomon Dinizulu [sic] and with other Zulu chiefs, has greatly gained in prestige amongst the natives in Durban . . . and that he, consequently, at present is a very much greater menace to Law and Order than he has ever been in the past.[59]

As we shall see, Commissioner of Police de Villiers was not the most perceptive observer of African politics, and his view that the ICU had become more inflammatory in tone was almost the opposite of the truth; nevertheless, it was his interpretation, rather than that of Durban's mayor, that held the day.

There were others besides the police urging Champion's removal. Most important of these was G. N. Heaton Nicholls, the M.P. for Zululand and the president of the South African and Zululand Planters' Union, whom we have already encountered as a key ideologue of segregation. Even before news of the rapprochement between Solomon and Champion hit the headlines, Nicholls was particularly concerned with what he saw as the discrepancy between the treatment accorded to the ICU activists, and the alleged disrespect of the administration for traditional authority. As he wrote to the minister of Native Affairs on 16 July 1930:

> The days of the assegai are over and the fears of a tribal combination under a Zulu paramount chief should be banished. There are more evil combinations under way which Chieftendom [sic] would assist us to fight against. . . . Because of his birth and the position in which we have placed him Solomon is regarded as the natural head of the Zulu race and whether he is officially recognised or not, he is so recognised by the natives themselves. . . . this refusal to recognise the natural leader of the Zulus tends to destroy the prestige of the Zulu chiefs as a whole. They are treated as so many village constables who dare not move

> without the permission of the local magistrate, whilst the agitator
> can move anywhere he likes. . . . I think it is pitiable that instead
> of strengthening our hold upon the aristocratic and conservative
> elements amongst the natives, we are driving them into the arms
> of native revolutionaries.[60]

Heaton Nicholls was exaggerating — the ICU organizers were hardly given a helping hand by local authorities anywhere in South Africa, and least of all in Natal — although he doubtless felt himself vindicated in his prognostications by the Durban meetings. This version of events did not go uncontested by the officials concerned, who defended their policies and denied that Solomon's recognition as king would check communism. Nevertheless, the Zululand politician and sugar baron's defense of the king and constant appeals for his recognition as a counter to "native revolutionaries" were significant, if somewhat ironic: after all, Nicholls was the spokesman of the very sugar planters in whose interests the power of Cetshwayo and Dinuzulu had originally to be broken. Nor was Heaton Nicholls alone. In 1928 a member of the Campbells of Mount Edgecombe, the eminent Natal sugar-planting family, similarly interviewed the minister of Native Affairs on the need to recognize Solomon as the "King of the Zulus."[61] The prosegregationist secretary for Native Affairs, J. S. Herbst, had little doubt as to the motives: "My impression is that the scheme suggested by Mr. Campbell is nothing more nor less than an attempt to get Solomon under the thumb of the employers of labour and to use him against the ICU."[62] It is perhaps no coincidence that Solomon's vigorous denunciations of the ICU had been to workers assembled on the Campbell sugar estates at Mount Edgecombe the previous year.

Solomon and the Zulu royal family were undoubtedly of direct utility to the employers of labor and not only to the sugar planters of Natal. According to Rebecca H. Reyher, who recorded the biography of Solomon's first wife, Christina Sibiya,

Solomon was a familiar figure to the mining industry. Frequently when unrest threatened he was sent for to address large gatherings of his people. In his honour thousands of natives sang and danced and gave an incomparable performance. . . . Unbelievably fantastic, truly magnificent, and inspiringly beautiful to the performers and others privileged to see it, this traditional expression of tribal unity served to counteract any seeds of rebellion. . . . Tribal organisation is of profound importance to the whole European economic structure and the head of the Zulu nation is therefore to be assiduously cultivated as the source of stable labour supply and a symbol of authority.[63]

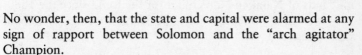

No wonder, then, that the state and capital were alarmed at any sign of rapport between Solomon and the "arch agitator" Champion.

There was a wider front, however, on which their fears were aroused. As a host of authors dealing with twentieth-century peasant revolutions have pointed out, for smouldering peasant discontent to flame into revolt, if not revolution, it is necessary in general for popular protest to fuse in some way with a more systematic, "derived" set of structured beliefs, beliefs that could transcend the parochialism and fragmentation inherent in peasant life. According to George Rudé, there are three elements in this process: the "inherent" popular beliefs; a "derived" or outside element of more structured and sophisticated beliefs, usually brought in by the literate bourgeoisie or petty bourgeoisie in peasant protest movements; and the circumstances and experience that "determined the nature of the final mixture."[64] It was precisely this fusion that the state and capital feared as they watched the impact of the ICU in the countryside and Champion's approaches to the chiefs and to Solomon. Certainly the "circumstances and experience" were ripe. Already by the time of the Bambatha Rebellion, land shortage had become a burning issue for Africans in many parts of Natal and was a major reason for that uprising, which had, however, a restorative rather than a revolutionary flavor to it.[65] Over the next decade matters deteriorated as white capitalist agriculture continued its almost phenomenal expansion in Natal, and the stratification of the landed and landless Africans increased apace. The impact of the 1913 Native Lands Act, although uneven, and the dramatic expansion of tropical plantation agriculture (sugar, wattle, cotton) in response to unprecedented world demand in the decade 1915 – 25 exacerbated the situation.

The impoverishment was clear to the labor recruiter and farmer J. W. McKenzie, who had been a landlord in the midlands of Natal and a recruiter for the Rand since the 1880s and who gave evidence before the Natal Shortage of Labour Committee in 1918:

> The natives are going from bad to worse. They are badly off now and don't get sufficient wages to pay their way. The ordinary Kaffir gets £1 a month, but with taxes, clothing and feeding his family the money won't go round. . . . They are growing less food. They have no manure in the kraal [i.e. homestead] and the land is cultivated year in and year out. I do not think 50% of the Natives in Natal grow enough for their own use. He is doing a lot less than he used . . . I have brought as many as 500 bags of mealies from one kraal years ago, but the position is changed. They had any amount of cattle and in those days the head of kraal was a man of importance; nowadays he is nothing — he has lost his status altogether. They were cattle breeders then; the question of labour was only a secondary consideration. Their living has gone now. I consider [that] at present they are in an impossible position. The only solution I can see [to the Natal labor shortage] is to pay them better wages.[66]

Paying them better wages was not the solution generally chosen by the employers of labor in Natal, whether on the farms, in the mines and plantations, or in the towns. In general, wage rates were somewhat lower and conditions very much worse than on the Rand — which is where those workers who could manage to accumulate sufficient resources to do so went. According to Champion, in Durban many Africans earned from £2 10s. to £4 a month without food and lodging, or from £1 10s. to £2 10s. with food and lodging supplied by the employer.[67] Rural wages were even lower, with wages per shift of only 1s. 4d. and 1s. 8d. At the mines in the Transvaal, the average wage per shift was approximately 2s. 2 1/4d., and although in both rural and mine work food, accommodation, and medical attention were provided, there is no doubt that provision at the gold mines was, by this time, greatly superior. For urban workers on the Rand, the most frequent wages ranged from £3 to £3 10s. for domestic and municipal workers, £4 6s. 8d. for industrial workers. As Maj. H. S. Cooke pointed out to the Native Economic Commission, all these wages were well below the minimum necessary for a family of four on the Witwatersrand, which he estimated at £6; the estimates from joint councils from other centers were very similar.[68]

In Zululand, the processes of proletarianization were somewhat more staggered; although labor migration probably began from Zululand with the destruction of the kingdom in the 1880s, proletarianization was still very uneven. Some of the southern districts were feeling stress by the beginning of the century; yet as late as 1925 magistrates could comment on the good year Africans had had, and the abundance of cattle and grain after the rains. In some areas, indeed, it was maintained that Africans had never been more prosperous.[69] One must be wary of taking these reports at face value. Though, as we have seen, in both Natal and Zululand there was a class of wealthy landowners, and some who had herds of two to four hundred in Zululand in the 1920s, they were undoubtedly the privileged few.[70]

For the majority, the effects of poverty and the changing nature of rural social relations were only too evident, as settler-owned cotton and sugar plantations expanded along the Zululand and Natal coastlands, and settler wattle and sheep farming spread in the thornveld of Zululand's interior and the northern and midland districts of Natal. Between 1924 and 1929, in Estcourt and Umvoti districts, for example, areas that became the scene of some of the most intense ICU activity, wattle plantations increased by over 500 percent, while the number of white-owned sheep doubled.[71] In the old republican districts of Vryheid, Utrecht, and Paulpietersburg — annexed to Natal after the South African War — rural social relations were dramatically restructured in the 1920s for the first time. All this meant increasing pressure on African lands, tightening restrictions on stock, intensified demands for labor and the transformation of former labor-tenancy arrangements as farmers took more land for their own production. The result was massive evictions.[72]

All over Zululand, the pressures were being felt. The ancient Chief Msigana Mtembu expressed the despair of his people before the 1930 – 32 Native Economic Commission:

> We have become a poor people through lack of something to sustain us. The land which we owned in the past has been taken from us by you here, and we have no cattle to speak of. . . . They have become just like scraggy dogs, and they are getting worse. . . . We have now exhausted the little land left to us, perhaps you can show us a way to climb to the sky, to develop there. . . . The people are wandering about the countryside looking for places . . . . You came along you defeated our king and took our land. For a short space of time we were left in peace, but that did not last long. . . . Now we find ourselves crowded out of all things. We are living most unhappily. . . . The inflictions which are being visited upon us are worse than I have ever known before. . . . Had we some place to fly to, to get away from all our troubles, we would follow that way. We are as good as dead as a people. We are hemmed in on all sides by farms.[73]

Chief Mgizo, grandson of the Zulu King Mpande, put it equally vividly when he talked of the evictions as the "yawning crack" which "empties forth human beings."[74] Many of these now "homeless wanderers"[75] found their way to Zululand where chiefs tried to squeeze them onto already overcrowded lands — lands that had seen a steady influx of Africans from Natal not only since the passage of the 1913 Lands Act but since the 1880s, when the British attempted to colonize southern Zululand with compliant Natal Africans.[76]

The effects in the coastal areas were different but no less traumatic. These areas of Zululand had always been sparsely populated — and with good reason. As the cotton and sugar plantations extended and the railway was built to service them, a malaria epidemic of major proportions raged. Virtually no health precautions were taken as non-immune labor was taken into areas of endemic malaria. The epidemic was not brought under control until the mid-1930s.[77] No wonder then that the whites "were accused of having introduced malaria into a Zulu arcady."[78]

It is against this background that the response of the Zulu to the spread of the ICU in the rural areas has to be understood. The move of the ICU headquarters to Durban and Johannesburg in 1926 led to "a proliferation of branches in the countryside,"[79] and as the *Times* (London) noted in October 1927, "thousands of Zulus are joining up. The red ticket of promise [i.e. the membership badge] is everywhere."[80] And it was among rural wage-tenants that ICU propaganda gained the most response.[81] As the ideas propagated by the small band of socialists and communists on the Rand and in Durban, and by the ICU's rural organizers, fused with popular consciousness, an almost millenarian expectation suffused the countryside. Popular resistance in the form of work stoppages and individual acts of defiance was transformed into a wave of strikes in which a 2,000 percent increase in wages (8s. a day) was demanded by labor-tenants, brandishing their red tickets and saying they would rather be shot than return to work.[82]

The reaction of the Natal farmers was immediate. At a Congress in 1927 they discussed the possibility of evicting ICU members from their farms — and proceeded to give their words effect.[83] Gilbert Coka, a young ICU organizer who later (briefly) joined the Communist party described what happened: "Throughout the countryside families were evicted in hundreds. Naturally they went to the ICU offices where they had been promised freedom. Farmers refused to have tenants who were members of the ICU. They spied them out, felling their huts to the ground, burning out others and throwing them to the roads, confiscating their stock if they did not leave quickly enough."[84]

The brutal evictions effectively crushed the wave of strikes. The refusal of the Labour-Nationalist coalition government to drastically change the law in order to deal with trade-unionists as summarily as the farmers would have liked and the failure of the law courts to underwrite the numerous evictions, however, further fuelled white farmer anger.[85] In 1928, ICU offices were burnt down in Bergville, Greytown, Weenen, Kranzkop and Pietermaritzburg. According to Coka:

> It was now a question of endurance. If the African would stand united for another twelve months, the fates of the landowners would be compromised, for their livelihood and prosperity was dependent on the semi-villeinage labour for which they hardly paid a farthing [labor-tenants in large areas of Natal were expected to work for six months for a wage that ranged between ten and thirty shillings — and sometimes simply the right to occupy a restricted amount of land]. . . . Africans were ready to do anything in order to throw off the chains of servitude and slavery. Everything rested with the higher officials [of the ICU]. A general strike, passive or even active resistance, demonstrations, or any militant move would, at the time, have changed the history of the Union. These masses were ready to follow the lead even to the death. The news of the outrages hardened their resolution to strive to the last. Everything depended on the leaders, and they gave no lead.[86]

Coka probably exaggerates the possible outcome. As we have seen the South African state has never been averse to using brute force when need be, and the divisions in the ruling class response would almost undoubtedly have been overcome had the threat to agrarian order extended. Whatever the nature of the leadership, Africans armed with sticks and stones were still no better prepared to face trained troops armed with machine guns in 1928 than in 1906. Yet there can be little doubt that a very substantial section of the peasantry had been radicalized; and this had its counterpart in the beer hall riot and demonstrations that we have already discussed, for town and countryside, urban and rural poor were and indeed, in much of South Africa, still are a single reality.

No wonder then that it was in the late 1920s that Heaton Nicholls began to formulate his program of revitalized segregation, and to advocate the restoration of the powers of the Zulu king. He expressed his fears of the communist menace very clearly in a series of letters written between 1929 and 1931, from which there has already been occasion to quote. Here a further couple of fragments must suffice. In May 1929 he wrote to J. H. Zutphen, "We must come back to the real essence of tribal life — communalism — a very different thing to communism. If we do not get back to communalism we will certainly arrive at communism. . . . We cannot long continue as a white aristocracy or black proletariat. . . . We end ultimately in the not too distant future in the class war."[87] In yet another letter around the same time, he set out his ideas on the ways to preempt class war even more explicitly: "The policy of a Bantu nation as distinct from that of a black proletariat — and that stripped of all verbiage, that is the real issue in Africa — obviously brings in its train a pride of race. The most race-proud man I know is Solomon. He glories in his race and its past prowess; and there is no native in the Union who is so earnestly desirous of maintaining a pure Bantu race purity."[88]

As it turned out, Coka's hopes and Heaton Nicholls's fears were equally misplaced. The possibility of a revolutionary consciousness being forged through the interaction of Champion and the oppressed workers and peasants was never wholly realistic. As the earlier outline makes clear, Champion's own position was replete with ambiguities; he was never the consistent revolutionary Heaton Nicholls would have us believe, and he openly and often attacked the Communists with whom he was supposed to be in league. As he remarked before the De Waal Commission of Enquiry into the Durban "riots":

> I know what Communism means, as I have studied the subject, and . . . I was sent to attend Communist meetings both by the Government and the Chamber of Mines. As a result of my study of the subject I have found that Communists are people who desire to change the existing system by which in Africa men like myself who hold landed properties should be dispossessed of them and these properties would be given to other people who have less than I have. In other words, those who have a lot should be dispossessed in favour of those who have little. That is where I disagree with Communism.[89]

That he should have disagreed with communism was hardly surprising. As a man of some property, Champion had little love for notions of share and share alike. In addition to his activities on behalf of the ICU in the 1920s, for which he was paid a monthly salary of twenty pounds, Champion had inherited a plot of land from his father in 1920 and owned a small sugar plantation; in tandem with the ICU, he published his own newspaper and ran a dance and meeting hall for profit; on top of this, he ran a business called the Vuka Africa Company and was "the sole partner" in a cooperative boot-repairing and tailoring establishment.[90] It may be true that "business was not his real interest" and that most of his commercial ventures were "marginal failures."[91] Despite his early union activities, however, the interests he fought for were communal and nationalist rather than of the working class.

While his own interpretations of his actions when applying to the Department of Native Labour for a passport were somewhat disingenuous, there was a certain measure of truth in his contention that he had

> contributed a great deal in assisting the natives to understand the administration better notwithstanding the fact that my claim may not be welcomed by some officials who know me as . . . a Native agitator. . . . I think when true History will finally be written by impartial observers my name shall be removed from that list and put in its proper place on the list of those who have done their best to have the white and black races live together as good friends.[92]

Whatever the white fantasies of his activities, Champion described his objectives on first coming to Natal in 1925 to James Laguma, assistant national secretary of the ICU, in similarly modest terms: "My whole aim, wherever I am, is to plead for the cause of the black man."[93] In July 1930 he suggested a meeting with the newly appointed Native Welfare Officer "to educate public opinion of both Europeans and Natives as to the advisability . . . of working together . . . in Durban for the welfare of both [and] that Mr. R [the Welfare Officer] should organise classes and lectures on the lines of the WEA between Europeans and Natives."[94] To Margery Perham, who visited South Africa from Oxford in 1929 in the course of a fact-finding African tour, he denied any intention of not wanting to cooperate with whites. On the contrary, he maintained:

> Miss, I do. But *they* will not co-operate; they will not even speak to a native. From the first to last in all our troubles here, has any official thought of asking the natives their opinion? . . . The Native Affairs officials in this city are absolutely unapproachable and unsympathetic. *Of course* I would co-operate. I know we cannot do without the whites in this country, but the whites will do nothing for us until we can organise and speak for ourselves. It is sympathy and understanding that we want.[95]

Now Champion was an infinitely complex individual, fully capable of adopting the necessary pose before officialdom or Oxford lady-scholars. Like Solomon and Dube, he was a master of the mask. According to the manifestly infuriated deputy commissioner of the South African police, S. J. Lendrum:

> Champion is known by those members of the Force who are intimately acquainted with him as a deep cunning scoundrel *very* clever and a wonderful actor. . . . Champion is a most smooth individual when spoken to by the police, and adopts a most child-like innocence when any reference is made to the unrest among the natives caused by his influence. . . . Champion will tell you, and makes a point of doing so, that he is out to do his utmost to help the Government and prevent any disturbances in any shape or form, yet whilst he is most careful in what he says and how he acts at meetings he will permit and support his Lieutenants in whatever they may say or do, be it ever so inflammatory.[96]

There is no doubt that Champion not infrequently adopted a populist rhetoric he was ill-prepared to defend in action; in addition to his protestations of innocence and alleged cooperativeness, he also said to Margery Perham that he "gloried in" the accusation that he was responsible for "poisoning the minds of his people against the Europeans" because "up till now, though they were oppressed, they did not understand why or by whom. Now, thanks to me every native in Durban knows. The only hope lies in discontent, because discontent produces organisation."[97] Despite this, however, Champion's actions throughout a long life characterized by political pragmatism and somewhat abrasive collaboration with both municipal and state authority support his claims to moderation. He, too, understood that colonial politics is the politics of the tightrope.

It is not my purpose here to discuss Champion's life after his return to Durban in 1934 in any detail. It included a long and complex career on the urban advisory councils set up by the government and on the executive of the All-African Convention formed to protest against the government's land and franchise legislation in 1936. He was also a member of the Native Representative Council and President of the Natal African Congress after Dube's death. Champion even took Dr. Xuma's place as acting president-general of the ANC in 1946 – 47, though his true base remained in the location politics of Durban. There, as Swanson remarks, "there seems little doubt that he would have gained first rank in the 'Chicago school' of big city favour-and-influence politics, had such opportunities been fully available to him."[98] From the thirties he retained his connection with the Zulu royal family. In his last years he corresponded regularly with Chief Gatsha Buthelezi, claiming to have originated, with Senator Cecil Cowley, the erstwhile ICU lawyer, the idea of the 'Bantu Investment Corporation', and urging Buthelezi to accept "independence" for Kwazulu.[99] He died in 1974, at the age of 82, still an active and controversial public figure.[100]

It is always difficult for the historian to plumb an individual's personal motivation. Rhetoric aside, however, what Champion seems to have wanted above all was personal power and its acknowledgment through consultation with the "other side" — in the 1920s, the Natal and Durban "native" administration. Thus, from his enquiry into the Durban "riots," Chief Justice de Waal believed that Champion's main grievance was that he had no right of approach to those he desired to interview.[101] While De Waal felt this was because Champion's "manner of approach was unfortunate to a degree,"[102] for the Durban authorities Champion's claims to social equality and demands for a living wage for Africans were in themselves revolutionary.[103] As late as April 1935, the native commissioner of Durban, G. P. Wallace, thought Champion's activities after his return from exile constituted a serious danger, because "he is a man whose main object in life is social equality with Europeans."[104] Wallace's successor as native commissioner, H. G. Arbuthnot, equally deplored the fact that

> Europeans in Durban who are interested in the uplifting and
> welfare of natives encourage rather than discourage their rapidly
> growing tendency of "social equality with Europeans." At
> meetings Europeans who should know better address natives as
> "Mr. Kanyile" or "Mr. Bhulose" as the case may be and actually
> shake hands with them, and to hear the natives addressing each
> other in the English language with the exphatic [sic] "Mr." prefix,
> is ludicrous.[105]

Clearly the position of *kholwa* Africans in Durban in the 1920s
and 1930s had changed little from 1908, when the local
populace was outraged when the new governor, Sir Matthew
Nathan, shook hands "with some Christian chiefs,"[106] and the
lines of *herrschaft* and hierarchy were as firmly drawn. Despite
its lip service to native welfare and the formation of the Native
Advisory Board, by and large the administration remained
unsympathetic to African aspirations and was only prepared to
deal with popular grievances through the authority of the chiefs
— on the assumption that all workers were only temporarily in
the city and could be controlled through their tribal authority.

Yet the Durban to which Champion had come in the
mid-1920s as ICU organizer hardly fitted this administrative
stereotype. A considerable number were, like Champion,
westernized and educated, anxious to make their way in the
world, even if, at present, they were forced to work as clerks
and messengers and drivers. Although Champion himself had
been radicalized on the Witwatersrand during the wave of
working-class militancy after World War I, there is little doubt
that his primary identification was with those he termed various-
ly "the intelligent class of natives," "the civilised class," and the
"better class of natives who own their own homes."[107] For this
group, the daily humiliations of Durban's administration and
the barriers to accumulation bit deeply. All over the country,
"scores of teachers, traders, clerks and craftsmen" flocked to
the standard of the ICU and formed its crucial second-level
leadership.[108] As Helen Bradford has pointed out, at a time

when the state was beginning to clamp down on the African elite and the color bar legislation was driving skilled artisans and craftsmen from state employment, they experienced a particularly powerful pull from those lower in the social scale. Their common experience of a racially defined land shortage, pass restrictions, and low wages was a powerful cement for their class alliance.[109]

If Dube and the landowners looked to the chiefs and the Zulu royal house as a conservative mode of mobilizing support, Champion and the Durban petty bourgeoisie needed wider support to achieve their aims. Their deeply felt populist and nationalist rhetoric served an important purpose with its stress on the solidarity of the people and its simultaneous denunciation of the exploitation of the workers by whites and their discrimination against black business. Although later in the century this was to spill over into intense anti-Indian feeling as well, at this stage these hostilities were muted. Class determinations were fluid in the extreme and in many ways the Durban petty bourgeoisie was as poorly off as many workers, and was subjected to the same daily degradation in terms of housing, police harassment, pass raids, and "deverminization"[110] as the migrant workers coming to Durban in increasing numbers in the 1920s. At every level conditions in Durban were appalling. The American missionary J. D. Taylor described the housing in Durban as, with some exceptions, "unfit for human habitation and there is better stabling for the horses than accommodation for the natives. Dark, unsanitary, without ventilation, they are absolute cess-pools of disease and evils of every kind."[111]

By comparison, for white observers, the municipal barracks for the so-called *togt* workers — the daily paid, unskilled laborers — may indeed have seemed "well constructed . . . clean, well kept and well ventilated. . . . a model which might well be emulated by other large urban centres" as Chief Justice de Waal alleged.[112] It is unclear whether black workers would have regarded this as sufficient recompense for the degree of social control the barracks exercised over their lives. Even including the barracks, however, in 1930 there was housing for only some 18,000 of Durban's 40,000 Africans, and married quarters for only 60 families.[113] Wages were low for all Africans, but while the migrants still had access to subsistence for their families in the countryside, increasingly, especially for the petty bourgeoisie, the rural base had disappeared. No wonder then that the scramble for petty entrepreneurial activity and the need to organize beyond the confines of their immediate class were critical.

Philip Bonner has described how on the Rand these conditions, combined with war-time inflation and the wave of militancy that spread among the working-class, radicalized the petty bourgeoisie in 1918 – 20. Drawing on Laclau's analysis of the ideological class struggle, Bonner argues that the petty bourgeoisie "lying between the two dominant relations of production, labour and capital, tended to swing according to the pressures exercised on it by the two contending parties." In the years after World War I, he suggests that the strength of working class militancy and action was such that it posed a severe crisis of commitment for the petty bourgeoisie. For a rare moment it split, and leading members united with the workers in mass action.[114]

In Durban the situation after World War I was less clear-cut. For a variety of reasons the city did not experience the wave of postwar working class action that swept most other South African towns; in most cases employers raised wages slightly before the workers took action, though they regarded the attempts of John Dube, who was at that time trying to act as spokesman for the workers and actively discouraging strike action, as particularly ominous.[115] In this sense, his position as intermediary was not dissimilar to that of Champion some seven or eight years later; their competition over a similar constituency in part accounts for the bitter enmity between the two.[116]

Through the twenties, the working class in Natal was weak,

isolated and fragmented. The largest concentrations of workers, other than labor-tenants and migrants on the farms, were at the coal mines of the Natal midlands and the coastal sugar plantations. Both these groups were desperately exploited and lacked leadership and organization. Wage rates and conditions at the coal mines and sugar plantations horrified even the Union government inspectors of native labour on their periodic inspections, as undercapitalized Natal owners tried to compete with the Rand for labor and on international markets for the sale of their commodities.[117] Yet Champion seemed uninterested in organizing the ICU on the plantations or at the scattered coal mines, despite the example set by Gandhi's spectacular passive resistance campaign and strike among Indian coal miners in 1913 and the efforts of his "lieutenants."[118]

Even where industrial unrest occurred, Champion, like Kadalie, was slow to take advantage of it. Thus in 1927, while he was deputy for Kadalie in Johannesburg, the ICU lost support "because of its inability . . . to take advantage of industrial unrest that occurred that winter."[119] In Natal, Champion was equally insensitive to the demands of the organized workers. Thus, a major strike of dockworkers to secure the release of workers who had been arrested for tax offenses in 1927 and the strike of over 4,500 coal miners in Newcastle were largely ignored by the union leader. As Champion pointed out to the Native Economic Commission in 1930, "One has to take grave risks to mix himself up with employed natives in the farms, sugar fields and mining industry"[120] — and on the whole the top organizers did not take these grave risks. It is easy to be critical in retrospect. It was in fact exceptionally difficult to gain access to workers at mines and plantations in the 1920s, and by and large the ICU organizers had neither the capacity nor the class consciousness to undertake it, though some of the lower-level agents were extremely active in the rural areas, as we have already seen.

Even in Durban itself, Champion's home-base, one can hardly

talk of a large industrial working class at this stage. Apart from some 2,000 dockworkers, in 1921 the largest single group of workers was the 7,127 Africans in domestic service, followed by 1,834 riksha pullers; the rest were split between a variety of small manufacturing and service establishments.[121] What united them all was the popular discontent arising from social conditions. This fragmentation in a sense underlay Champion's strategy in Durban. His strategy was not directed by a working-class action designed to improve wages and conditions for large groups of workers; the issues he took up were either at the level of the individual worker, or were popular issues that afflicted the petty bourgeoisie as harshly as the workers. The strategy made eminent sense, not because of some innate conservatism or vested interest of the petty bourgeoisie, but because of the fragmented and ambiguous nature of class formation and class consciousness at the time. As we have already seen, in Durban even the petty bourgeoisie lived on the margins of poverty and suffered the indignities of racial oppression. As Helen Bradford has remarked, the pressures on the petty bourgeoisie at this time meant that "it was extremely susceptible to proletarianisation." For Champion, as for the ICU leaders and officials more generally, "the probability of being extruded as a wage-earner was considerably greater than that of emerging as a capitalist," so that "many who had scrambled into wage employment were capable of articulating worker demands spontaneously." At the same time, the "devastating blows dealt by the Pact government" on African craftsmen, teachers, clerks, and skilled workers and the failure of either white liberals or African nationalist organizations to protect them "made downward rather than upward alliances increasingly attractive."[122]

For all his populist rhetoric and preparedness to speak on behalf of Durban's workers, however, Champion remained anxious to distinguish himself from his clientele. Despite his early contacts with the Communist party in Johannesburg, and unlike many of his fellow organizers in the ICU, he was hardly imbued with any revolutionary consciousness that the capitalist system itself was oppressive and needed to be rejected. On the contrary, through a variety of entrepreneurial activities Champion was very busily trying to make the capitalist system work for him. What he wanted was the freedom to compete with whites and Indians in it; this did not preclude his having a genuine sense of the grievances of the urban and rural poor, and a desire to act as their spokesman, a role that was both needed and appreciated by disorganized and illiterate workers.

The case was somewhat different, however, with the dockworkers. The dockworkers constituted the major exception to the disorganization of the working class in Durban, and they almost proved Champion's undoing. As Dave Hemson has shown, they were the most militant branch of Durban's working population, with their first strike action going back to the last third of the nineteenth century.[123] This is all the more remarkable because they were mainly *togt*, or daily-paid casual labor. Nevertheless, they were all housed in a single area at the Point in easy reach of the harbor, and the town, and this certainly facilitated their mobilization. For while they could develop their own internal organizational forms at the barracks, they were also able to attend the various socialist and ICU meetings being held in Durban in the twenties. Here, again, there was indeed the fusion that the state so feared between popular protest and the ideologies of the intelligentsia.

Paradoxically, however, it was the militancy this inspired that threatened Champion's position and left him, after the beer-hall riots of 1929, vulnerable and exposed. Thus, the dockworkers who continued the beer boycott, demanded higher wages, and were in the forefront of resistance to increased taxation further embarrassed Champion, who had no desire to engage in head-on confrontation with the state. Throughout his life, Champion had a realistic sense of the dangers of violence unleashed by the ruling-class in response to working-class action. Not only had he witnessed the Bambatha Rebellion in 1906; he had vivid recollections of the police action against black workers in 1920 in Johannesburg and perhaps even more dramatically of the state action against white workers in 1922.[124] As he remarked to an interviewer late in his life, "I don't believe in a policy of awaking the sleeping dogs when they can bite you and you are not armed."[125] This caution guided his decision to "calm" the crowd on behalf of the chief of police, and also his turn to find alternative allies by the end of 1929.

This was made more urgent because the breakaway of the Durban branch of the ICU after Champion's suspension from the national organization in 1928 had led to widespread disillusion with the ICU in the rest of Natal. The evicted peasantry were particularly bitter. The rank and file simply ceased paying their membership dues, and some even demanded their money back.[126] Without funds to pursue his old tactic of legal action or to pay officials, the beerhall boycott had been a last-minute attempt to regain popularity; in fact, it simply increased his difficulties, as the arrest of six of his officials imposed further high court fees and fines on the union. His attempts to find funds in Johannesburg were unsuccessful, as were his discussions with Kadalie in the hopes of healing the breach between the different fragments of the ICU.[127] As African workers were increasingly mobilized behind the dynamic Communist party leadership in Durban in 1930, Champion, confronted with a desperate need for funds, began to look for a safer rural base and alternative ways of presenting what he conceived as the African case.

As he wrote to the president and governing body of the ICU Yase Natal in February 1930, he now began to pay "certain attention to organising the Native Chiefs in Natal and Zululand," a strategy he and Kadalie had both flirted with unsuccessfully as early as 1928. Now however he claimed that he was succeeding "in winning the favour of many hitherto opposed to the ICU. . . . The greatest question is to get these people to contribute to our funds," which were at an even lower ebb, as he had failed to receive any compensation for the destruction of the organization's property.[128] According to the deputy commissioner of the South African police, by June 1930 Champion had

> lost a good deal of control, power, and influence amongst the native community in Durban, and he is now frantically striving to regain lost ground . . . [by inducing] certain chiefs from outside to come to and take an interest in his meetings. . . . Champion's sole object in getting the Chiefs interested is to magnify himself in the eyes of the Durban natives who, when they see their Chiefs present or interested naturally become impressed with Champion's importance.[129]

It was in this context that Champion began the overtures to Solomon that so worried Heaton Nicholls and the state. Paradoxically, it was his search for respectability and a more conservative constituency rather than his leadership of the Durban working class that seemed to carry the most revolutionary potential for the state and that finally provoked the minister of justice into banishing him from Natal in September 1930.

CHAPTER 4

Conclusions

A profound ambiguity still remains. From the ways in which the state and the sugar planters, Dube, and Champion all turned in their moments of crisis to the Zulu royal family and the ideology it provided, it is clear that Solomon still had very real powers. That they were successfully utilized lends support to Poulantzas' view that "dominant ideology does not simply reflect the conditions of existence of the dominant class . . . but rather the concrete relations between the dominant and dominated classes."[1] The Zulu royal family still had a powerful grip on the popular imagination, notwithstanding an increasing radicalization of African peasants and workers and notwithstanding the fact that the king had few material powers any longer and lived off the tribute he could still exact from the people. (The very fact that he could still exact it with little, if any, material coercive machinery reinforces the point). Nor was this grip purely ideological. Given the nature of partial proletarianization in South Africa, for both peasant and migrant laborer there was a continued material reality (at least in this period) in social and political relations in the countryside. Chiefs still had considerable power over the daily lives of their subjects, and it is this, in part, that explains the retention among migrants of the ideology of the precapitalist social formation.

In this ideology, despite — and, perhaps, because of — conquest, the king remained symbolically central. In the Zulu state, as we have seen, he had ideally represented the unity of the

13. *Chief Gatsha Buthelezi at Shaka Day Celebrations in "traditional garb"* (UNISA Africana Collection).

14. *Chief Buthelezi with fellow Bantustan leaders, Chiefs Mangope and Matanzima* (UNISA Africana).

15. *Chief Buthelezi with Prince Zwelitheni Goodwill* (UNISA Africana collection).

community, its father and redistributor. He and his ancestors were believed to ensure the integrity and well-being of the people. At a time of growing exploitation, when subordinate chiefs were increasingly coming to be seen as subservient to white demands, what could be more natural than that the people should turn to the king for protection — a common enough phenomenon in preindustrial protest.[2] Certainly Max Gluckman saw it in this way in the thirties. At a time when the subordinate chiefs were becoming increasingly unpopular through their abuse of power, he argued, the king "had no power to abuse"; he could continue to express national sentiment, and precisely because of the state's obduracy in failing to recognize him, people could express their resentment against white rule through their allegiance to the Zulu royal family.[3]

For John Dube and the *kholwa* landowners, the Zulu monarchy afforded a different kind of opportunity. In an era of segregation, the disillusion with nineteenth-century ideals of assimilation and progress and the recognition of the need to find a new constituency, and "a new way of linking fraternity, power and time meaningfully together," led to the creation of a new "cultural artefact,"[4] namely, an ethnic nationalism that coexisted in ambiguous fashion with the older, broader pan – South African black nationalism and with new forms of class consciousness. The rich historical and cultural tradition of the Zulu and the continued reality of this tradition in popular consciousness assisted the *kholwa* in their ideological labor, but it did not in itself predict that a Zulu ethnic nationalism would be constructed. For as Elizabeth Colson was perhaps the first to point out, contemporary African "tribal groupings" are not simply "survivals from the precolonial political world, though they may seek to acquire legitimacy through a myth of ancient unity. . . . They are not grass roots movements springing from the genius of the people. . . . They are largely the conscious creations of intellectuals and other active leaders who have had the greatest opportunity to participate in the larger political and social world."[5]

As we have seen, intense social dislocation was a potent spur to the construction of a local political community centered around the king, for the *kholwa* petty bourgeoisie as well as for mine magnates, sugar barons, and certain elements in the state. It is perhaps no coincidence that James Stuart, assistant magistrate of Durban in the early years of this century, who was keenly concerned with what he saw as the dangers of "detribalisation" (i.e. proletarianization) and the undermining of "the discipline of tribal life," was the first systematic recorder of Zulu "oral tradition" and the author of a series of vernacular histories of the Zulu people and their warrior kings.[6] Their popularity as school readers may have partly assisted in the legitimation for the intelligentsia of their ethnic nationalism. Thus, from being a threat to the colonial order, Zulu history and the Zulu monarchy became a crucial part of the strategy of social control.

One can, I think, go further, but I introduce the next thought with due hesitation. It is always difficult to explore popular consciousness, and the perceptions held by the masses of the people in Natal and Zululand are far from clear, especially as those perceptions were reported and refracted through largely hostile colonial officials on the one hand or through the literate African elite and the far-from-disinterested royal family on the other. Nevertheless, it does seem to me that we have to be alert to the possibility that though the form — identification with the Zulu royal family — remained the same, the actual content of the ideology had changed. For while it is true that as societies undergo rapid social change, older ideological elements are taken up into the new situation, they are also transformed in the process.[7] Ernesto Laclau points to this, I think, when he suggests that although migrants to the city inevitably bring with them "the symbols and ideological values of the society from which they come," we should be careful how we interpret this:

Superficially this would appear to be the survival of old elements, but in reality, behind this survival is concealed a transformation: these rural elements are simply the raw material which the ideological practice of the new migrant transforms in order to express new antagonisms. In this sense, the persistence of certain ideological elements *can* [I would prefer *may*] express exactly the opposite of traditionalism: a refusal to accept capitalist legality."[8]

In the South African, or the Natal, case there seems to me to be one further twist. Because the majority of workers in Natal were not — and still are not — one-way migrants, but part of an institutionalized migrant labor system, and because the state itself was attempting to take over part of the political and ideological discourse of the subordinated, precapitalist, social formations to create some kind of hegemony for itself, there was a fundamental ambiguity at the heart of the popular support for the *herrschaft* of the Zulu royal family. We have already witnessed this both when Solomon attempted to recruit for the Native Labour Contingent during World War I and at the Nongoma meeting. And this explains Max Gluckman's observation in the late 1930s that in the towns "even demonstrations of loyalty to the King . . . have been marked by some show of hostility."[9] If the people looked to the king to protect them against the oppression of the state, they also looked to the state to protect them against the exactions of the king.

Paradoxically, moreover, as the central state achieved its ambition against the parochial fears of Natal, and the royal family was granted increased recognition, so the monarchy's utility in restabilizing social relations has declined. Today, although Solomon's nephew, Gatsha Buthelezi, the chief minister of Kwazulu, can still call on a generalized loyalty to the Zulu royal family to sustain his own similarly dependent *herrschaft*, he has to combine in his discourse a variety of other popular ideological elements. And although the state has attempted to elevate the powers of the current hereditary king of the Zulu, Goodwill, it has had little success in the face of his ineffectuality and unpopularity, which has simply been increased by the state's attentions.

These essays have dwelt in their detail on a period of more than fifty years ago. Yet my choices of individual and episode were not random. They have their resonance in recent events in South Africa, not because I am "burdened by the present,"[10] but because I share with *History Workshop Journal* the view that history "not only enables one to understand the past, but also offers the best critical vantage point from which to view the present."[11]

Let me in closing, then, turn briefly to Kwazulu, the impoverished and fragmented "self-governing" bantustan created by the South African state out of the "African" areas of Zululand and Natal — the reserves and locations and African freehold lands whose genesis we have been looking at. (It should be noted that no such "Indistan" has been proposed for Natal's 665,000 Indian inhabitants.) As the 1982 Buthelezi Commission on "the requirements for stability and development in Kwazulu and Natal" points out, "on average the region of Kwazulu and Natal is poorer in terms of output per head than is the Republic as a whole and within the region Kwazulu is very much poorer than Natal."[12] Although there are a number of small African sugar planters, who are in many ways the ideological successors of the men of Ifafa and Groutville whom Dube exhorted in 1927, the land fails to provide subsistence for more than a tiny fraction of its de facto, let alone its de jure, population.[13] Annual per-capita income in Kwazulu in 1980 was under R200; of this only R45 came from domestic production.[14] Its division into forty-four separate patches of land makes any planning for "development" a nightmare.

From a situation in which the rural areas subsidized the welfare costs of the migrant laborer, today the vast majority of the inhabitants of Kwazulu are dependent on the earnings of migrants and commuters to the "white economy" for subsistence. Yet 80 percent of these earnings are spent in the area of the "white economy."[15] Kwazulu is a land of "women without men," as each year about two-thirds of the able-bodied men seek work at the mines, farms, and factories of white South Africa.[16] Increasingly, it is also becoming a land of children without parents: migrants from Kwazulu have been leaving at an increasingly young age, in larger numbers, and for longer periods of time, and recently there has been a sharp rise also in the number of women forced to migrate in search of a basic subsistence. Starved of capital, there is no industry to provide local employment, and in some regions the absentee rate of men between the ages of twenty and forty-five is 80 percent, while 50 percent of the population is under the age of fifteen.[17]

Through the sixties and early seventies, the South African state was intent on streamlining the bantustans as labor reserves. Through a complex system of labor bureaus, pass laws and call-back cards, the state hoped to control the distribution of African labor. Bantustans like Kwazulu were intended to serve as the site of South Africa's industrial reserve of the unemployed, as well as of the old and the very young, who could be drawn into and thrown out of the economy according to its demands and at little immediate cost to whites. Increasingly, however, these functions have broken down as the desperately poor have streamed to the towns in search of work regardless of the consequences. In 1980, over a quarter of the workforce in Kwazulu was unemployed.[18] Today, huge, "illegal" shantytowns of people in an endless search for work ring the so-called white cities of Durban and Pietermaritzburg in Natal. There are similar agglomerations around Cape Town, Pretoria, and the towns of the Rand.

It is on the labor of countless black migrants, in whose organization the Zulu royal family played so important a role, that South Africa's capitalist development has been built. As elsewhere in the southern African periphery, dire poverty and dependence have led to and been exacerbated by the constant drain of the able-bodied and energetic from the rural areas.

Epidemic disease and malnutrition are rife and infant mortality several times that of whites.[19] Although the paramountcy of the Zulu kings is now recognized by the state, and the king has assumed the role of constitutional monarch that John Dube had so ardently requested, the dependence of both the king and his people on the South African state has never been more profound. The Kwazulu government relies on the central South African government for some three-quarters of its revenue and most of its investment.[20] The contrast between past glory and present poverty could not be starker.

Chief minister of this poverty-stricken labor reserve is Gatsha Buthelezi, a man who embodies in his contradictory position all the ambiguities of a Solomon, a Dube, a Champion. The son of Princess Magogo, daughter of Dinuzulu and sister of Solomon, and Matole Buthelezi, grandson of Cetshwayo's chief councillor, Gatsha Buthelezi was educated at the University College of Fort Hare, where he was a member of the African National Congress Youth League in the 1940s and early 1950s. In 1953, he returned to become chief of the Buthelezi people and adviser to King Cyprian; his skillful resistance to the imposition of the Bantustan policy in Zululand successfully thwarted government plans for several years, and ultimately forced a change in the legislation. Thus he established a reputation as a major opponent of apartheid and a fearless champion of African interests.

With the change in the law in 1972, however, he maintained that he no longer had any choice and reluctantly accepted that he had to work within the system. He did this, as he put it, "not because we believe in apartheid as a philosophy, but because there being no alternative allowed, it was in the interests of a peaceful settlement of South Africa's problems that we do so."[21]   Aware of the appalling poverty and demand for land in Kwazulu, and the absurd fragmentation of his domain, Buthelezi has refused to accept "independence" as offered by the South African state unless the government agrees to the consolidation of the Zulu "homeland" and the addition of further land to its domain. The government's as-yet-unfulfilled consolidation proposals of 1975 allocated a mere 38 percent of the land in Natal and Zululand for 77 percent of the population.[22] Even the state's modest consolidation proposals, which would reduce Kwazulu's forty-four segments to ten, are, however, fiercely resisted by Natal's white farmers and sugar magnates. Yet as long as Kwazulu refuses to accept "independence," the South African government's efforts to redefine its African population as "citizens" of "national homelands" and thus create a white majority in the Republic are thwarted. Even if every other ethnic group accepts independence, there will be an African majority inside "white" South Africa.

As a scion of its house, Buthelezi has been enmeshed in the Byzantine intrigues of Zulu royal family politics since childhood. His own succession to the chieftaincy of the Buthelezi people was not uncontested and for most of his adult years he has felt beset by enemies and spies, both black and white. While declaring his loyalty to the throne, he is a firm believer that his cousin the king should remain a constitutional monarch, above politics. Thus in 1972 when Kwazulu was vested with the status of a "Territorial Authority," he made quite sure that the king was not given the power to appoint the chief councillor or "prime minister": "Zulus love their king," he wrote at the time, "and it is unthinkable that he should be given executive functions which mean inevitable involvement in politics. . . . which would tarnish the royal image."[23]

In 1972, Buthelezi became the first chief minister of the new Territorial Authority of Kwazulu, with a not-ungenerous salary from the South African state. In 1975, he resurrected the *Inkatha* National Cultural Liberation Movement, modeled on Solomon and Dube's earlier example, an organization with lofty ideals of inculcating a spirit of unity among "the people of Kwazulu throughout Southern Africa, and between them and all their African brothers in Southern Africa."[24] But this organization quite quickly acquired a reputation for violent vigilante action against its opponents and for provision of "special favors" for its members. Unlike the earlier organization, Buthelezi's *Inkatha*, a brilliant meld of the old and the new, rapidly acquired the political muscle to give its leader standing well beyond his local community. By 1980, *Inkatha* was said to have 300,000 paid-up members, most of them rural, and 95 percent Zulu-speaking.[25]

There are direct continuities between the old *Inkatha* and the new. As the chief minister pointed out in 1977 when he opened Mr. Edward Ngobese's supermarket in Eshowe:

> Mr. Ngobese Senior is a great patriot whose committment [*sic*] to his people dates back over many decades. During the reign of King Solomon when the old Inkatha was still in existence, he was its staunch member. Some years ago when I was in the forefront of efforts to found the present Inkatha Mr. Ngobese gave the idea his full support. . . . When we launched 'Inkatha yenkululeko Yesizwe' . . . both Mr. R S Ngobese [senior] and his son, were with us.[26]

"For Blacks," Buthelezi continued, "success in a venture of this kind, amounts to success for the whole nation." Despite reference in the speech to the obstacles in the way of black development through racial discrimination and land shortage and to the plight of the unemployed and the dangers this posed,[27] among his concerns were the virtues of self-help and the service black businessmen rendered the community. Increasingly, Buthelezi appears to represent the small class of African accumulators, the chiefs and wealthier landowners, the new black businessmen and sugar farmers in Kwazulu, as well as a certain number of professionals. This is essentially the group that sees its class interests sustained within the Bantustan "state," rather than, as would appear to be the case with his opponents among the students at Ngoye and the Durban Medical School, in the wider South African arena.[28] His concerns mirror those of the aspirant bourgeoisie and petty bourgeoisie, although their class interests are masked by his claims to speak on behalf of "my people" and the need to "temper" the harshness of unfettered capitalism with the humanity of African communalism.

Yet, like Dube, Buthelezi attempts to court both the national African petty bourgeoisie and his Natal constituency, the former through the colors, songs, and slogans of the African National Congress and his refusal to accept "independence," the latter through *Inkatha* and its ethnic nationalism. In the seventies, he could count on considerable support from both, although the Black Consciousness Movement was an early critic. Since 1979, the dramatic reorganization of the trade unions and the remarkable resurgence of both working class activity and the African National Congress in South Africa have sharpened and radicalized politics, and his position has become somewhat less secure.[29] While still espousing a pan – South African nationalism, and the creation of a common society in the language of the African National Congress, he is increasingly dependent on his local constituency and its ethnic symbolism.[30]

Also like Dube, who operated in the oppressive and repressive context of the Bambatha Rebellion, the 1913 Lands Act, and a "refurbished traditionalism," Buthelezi is caught in the almost intolerable situation of apartheid in South Africa. He is fully aware of the futility of opposing the might of the South African state with slogans and stones, as in Soweto in 1976: he is distanced from the radicalized ANC and repudiates the notion of armed struggle. The lessons of Bambatha have endured. So have the messages of John Dube, to whom Buthelezi paid fulsome tribute in 1974 as "a man who was not only one of the most prominent leaders of the Zulu people, but one of the greatest leaders of the African people in South Africa during his life-time. . . . he was a man who believed in grass-roots upliftment of his people. He could be a peasant among peasants as well as an Academic amongst academicians, and a politician who was a statesman amongst politicians."[31]

In his encomium to Dube, Buthelezi explicitly compared Dube's interests in education with his own: "like him, I, too, have my heart centered mainly in the education of my race."[32] At the same time he places a high premium on "law and order." Like Dube, Buthelezi is trapped uncomfortably into trying to address his polarized audiences in words of moderation and modernization, and continues to propagate the values of liberalism, a Christian universalism, and ethnic nationalism, while allying himself, as did Dube, with big capital and its political representatives in the Progressive Federal party, with whose members he has frequently shared a political platform.[33] Advocating free enterprise and opposing the international campaign of disinvestment against South Africa, Buthelezi is seen by many as the only hope of peaceful settlement in South Africa. Yet the contradictions between Buthelezi's portrayal of himself as the man of peace and conciliation and the activities of some of his *Inkatha* agents were clear, in 1980, at the time of the African schools boycott in the Durban location of KwaMashu (by the logic of the apartheid state part of Kwazulu). While vigilantes of *Inkatha* assaulted the schoolchildren, Buthelezi blamed ANC and "non-Zulu agitators," rather than state policies, for the violence and threatened the pupils with expulsion if they did not return to their classrooms. In his view, even education for inferiority was better than no education.[34]

If Buthelezi resembles Dube in his constituency and his condemnation of popular action that he does not directly control, then he shares with Champion, a man he knew well and learned from despite the differences between them, a reputation for not controlling the strong-arm tactics of his followers on occasion. Like Champion, too, he is not averse to using a deliberately threatening populist rhetoric. He frequently warns his white and Indian audiences of the warlike potential of his Zulu regiments, and the bloodshed to come if there are no significant concessions to blacks, although he usually couples this with a caution to his followers to act with restraint. Typical were his remarks in a conference of the eight "Bantustan" leaders with the prime minister, B. J. Vorster, and minister of Bantu administration and development, M. C. Botha in January 1975:

> I would like to make it crystal-clear that I am not saying these things in any spirit of ill-will or threats, but I feel that it is my moral duty at this point in time, to point out, the only logical alternatives we now have, if we do not want our people to resort to Civil disobedience and disruption of services in this land. Not that I intend leading my people in this direction at the moment, but I feel judging by the mood of my people, that it is timely, that I should point out that if no meaningful change is forthcoming for them through the government's policies this will come as a logical alternative.[35]

More recently, following the white South African referendum on the government's constitutional proposals, which excluded the majority of Africans from the electoral system established for Indians and coloureds, he warned whites, and perhaps especially the supporters of the constitution in the Progressive Federal party, that "it might be possible for Inkatha to form a 'marriage of convenience' with the ANC and PAC," the externally based South African national liberation movements.[36]

Like Champion, too, he employs a populist rhetoric in attempting to mobilize a working-class audience and couples demands for human rights and a living wage, though his agents have hardly been concerned with serious workplace organization. Quick to criticize the intervention of the king in labor relations during strikes in Durban in 1973, he is more anxious to gain support of national and international capital for his plans for Kwazulu development than to challenge the structures of exploitation confronting workers in Kwazulu. When, in the early seventies, the minister of labor in the Kwazulu government, Barney Dladla, seemed too successful in promoting worker rights, he was rapidly replaced.[37]

The analogies are perhaps closest between Buthelezi and

Solomon, although quite manifestly the former is also a far more formidable leader, with a competence, intellect, and personal charisma that the self-indulgent Solomon never possessed. He is also able to deliver resources to his constituency that the constantly impecunious Solomon would have envied. To an even greater extent than Solomon, in his political maneuvering Buthelezi is able to draw on the rhetoric and symbolism both of his Zulu ancestry and of the pan – South African nationalist movement — something neither men would have seen as contradictory. Preceded by his royal bard, or *imbongi*, singing his praises in terms redolent of the heroic past, Buthelezi conjures with past and present in ways few African leaders, with the possible exception of the late King Sobhuza of Swaziland, can emulate. And while the ideological labor of his *imbongi* creates "an illusion of heroism, grandeur and achievement which clouds and distracts from present realities," it also provides, as Liz Gunner has pointed out, "powerful inspiration for the present . . . a much needed sense of continuity and . . . an image of achievement and strength with which people can identify."[38]

Far more formidably than Solomon, Buthelezi is simultaneously a potential threat to the state and indispensable to it. By refusing to accept the "independence" being foisted on the other Bantustan leaders, Buthelezi has seriously disrupted the plans of the government. As his praise poem puts it, he is the "Buffalo that stared fiercely at the constitution of the Kwazulu government, / all were afraid to challenge."[39] His outspokenness has led to several attempts by the South African state to destabilize his position, especially through the establishment of alternative political organizations, backed by other members of the royal family. And there is little evidence that members of the National party government enjoy his close relationship with their political opponents or his addresses to an international audience from a stage they have themselves constructed. Yet, they cannot simply get rid of him. To ban a Bantustan leader, particularly one of Buthelezi's stature, would undoubtedly raise more difficulties for the state than it would solve. He thus constantly faces the state with his contradictory presence both as critic and collaborator extraordinary; and, as in the case of Solomon, he is simultaneously needed and feared. His very criticism lends the apartheid structures a legitimacy no mere stooge could confer, at the same time as the apartheid structures themselves give him the platforms from which he is able to criticize the government, both at home and abroad.[40]

As we have seen, in the 1920s Heaton Nicholls and big capital saw the Zulu monarchy and "Bantu communalism" as the answer to "Bantu communism." So today, in the face of the increasing social dislocation resulting from apartheid and the heightened challenges to it, the Progressive Federal party and large-scale national and international capital, all of whom fear the rise of radical and more militant popular movements, see Buthelezi as the "Key to White Hopes,"[41] "white South Africa's best chance."[42] Indeed, in what some authors have seen as the current crisis of legitimacy for the South African state, the reformists in the National party, who are attempting to widen the basis of the state and find ways of incorporating at least sections of the black middle class and skilled workers, are also turning to Buthelezi. Unlike the other Bantustan leaders, Buthelezi is not simply dependent, then, on government favor. As Saul and Gelb remark, what distinguishes him is the way in which "he has chosen his constituency carefully, with an investor's eye to the long haul . . . . he seeks to place himself on offer as the guarantee of 'reform,' as an insurance policy against the risks entailed in the shift from racial to liberal capitalism, as a man for all 'national conventions' and all power-sharing schemes."[43]

But times have quite clearly changed. Despite the similarities in the positions of a Buthelezi, a Solomon, a Dube, a Champion, it would be wrong to push these comparisons beyond an understanding of the way in which structural complexity produces contradiction, although there may be elements in Zulu cultural heritage that enable these contradictions to be played out in a popularly understood idiom of ambiguity.[44] Both the structural complexities and the ambiguities have changed. The development of both working-class and national consciousness — and the two are not necessarily unconnected — is marked when the 1970s and 1980s are compared with the 1920s. With the growing power of the black trade unions, and the development of a self-conscious working class with an increasingly experienced and sophisticated leadership drawn from their own ranks, workers in Natal no longer turn to a Dube or a Champion — or even a Buthelezi — to articulate their grievances. At the same time, the changed geopolitical situation in southern Africa, as surrounding states acquired their independence in the 1970s, and the resurgence of African nationalism in a variety of forms in South Africa bring a new volatility and unpredictability to the region.

Although in the late 1970s Buthelezi's support both within Kwazulu and more generally in South Africa was high, it was never unconditional; it, too, has its ambiguities. Like Solomon, his popularity is directly dependent on not being seen to be too closely allied to the white power bloc. If in Solomon's case popular responses can only be imperfectly gauged through official reports of hostile meetings, the ups and downs of Buthelezi's popularity are charted in minute detail by the self-interested opinion polls of the international and national media. Undoubtedly, in the presence of the rising tide of black militancy, the options open to Buthelezi have narrowed considerably. Like his royal predecessor he walks a tightrope; indeed, he is a master of the art. Yet, at moments when he comes to be seen as the manifest agent of white control, his credibility with an increasingly militant black constituency even in Kwazulu is immediately undermined, as the polls show. If he errs in the opposite direction, in the final analysis the South African state could intervene, although both Buthelezi and the government are well aware of the heavy price that would have to be paid. Although over the past couple of years his lambasting of other leaders and his hostility to the liberation movements have affected his popularity, it would be unwise to underrate the force of his newly recreated and reinforced ethnic nationalism or his capacity to manipulate the elements of ambiguity in the current and coming struggles.

Appendix

GENEALOGY OF THE ZULU KINGS

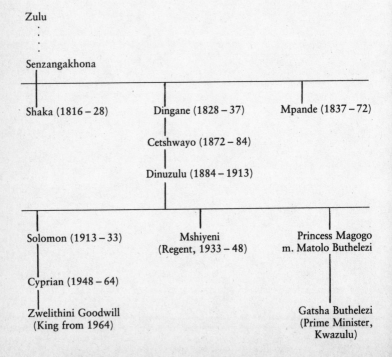

Zulu
⋮
Senzangakhona

Shaka (1816 – 28) Dingane (1828 – 37) Mpande (1837 – 72)

Cetshwayo (1872 – 84)

Dinuzulu (1884 – 1913)

Solomon (1913 – 33) Mshiyeni (Regent, 1933 – 48) Princess Magogo m. Matolo Buthelezi

Cyprian (1948 – 64)

Zwelithini Goodwill (King from 1964) Gatsha Buthelezi (Prime Minister, Kwazulu)

Notes

Preface

1. I am grateful to Professor Coralie Bryant for allowing me to modify a phrase that she and Louise White first used in an unpublished paper, "Dilemmas of Dependency: Leadership in the District of Columbia," Washington, D.C., 1973.
2. William Empson, *Seven Types of Ambiguity* (London, 1930), xx.
3. Introduction to Shula Marks and Richard Rathbone, eds., *Industrialisation and Social Change in South Africa: African Class Formation, Culture and Consciousness, 1870 – 1930* (London, 1982).

Introduction

1. Neville Hogan, "The posthumous vindication of Zachariah Gqishela," in Shula Marks and Anthony Atmore, eds., *Economy and Society in Pre-Industrial South Africa* (London, 1980), 277.
2. Steve Biko, "Fear — an important determinant in South African Politics," in Steve Biko, *I Write What I Like* (London, 1978), 78.
3. Max Gluckman, *Analysis of a Social Situation in Modern Zululand*, Rhodes Livingstone Papers, no. 28, 1940 – 42 (reprinted, Manchester, 1968), 25.
4. John W. Cell, *The Highest Stage of White Supremacy: The Origins of Segregation in South Africa and the American South* (Cambridge, 1982), 22.
5. See, for example, Stanley B. Greenberg, *Race and State in Capitalist Development: Comparative Perspectives* (New Haven, 1980); George M. Frederickson, *White Supremacy: A*

Comparative Study on American and South African History (New York, 1981); Howard Lamar and Leonard Thompson, *The Frontier in History: North America and Southern Africa Compared* (New Haven, 1982). For a work not explicitly comparative, but influenced by the recent work on South Africa, see Eric Foner, *Nothing but Freedom: Emancipation and Its Legacy* (Baton Rouge, 1983).

6. Cell, *Origins of Segregation*, 14.

7. Ibid., ix, 15.

8. Ibid., x, 18.

9. Ibid., 19.

10. Ibid., chap. 2.

11. Frederickson, *White Supremacy*, 241.

12. These last two paragraphs encapsulate my criticisms of John Cell's otherwise admirable *Origins of Segregation*.

13. I owe this insight, and the quoted phrase, to Professor David Cohen. I deal with this aspect of Dube's life in my original article, "The Ambiguities of Dependence: John L. Dube of Natal," *Journal of Southern African Studies* 1, no. 2 (1975): 165 – 6.

14. For a structuralist account that has left little space for human actors, see Robert H. Davies, *Capital, State and White Labour in South Africa, 1900 – 1960* (Brighton, 1979); for the unsatisfactory nature of the literature on African nationalism, see the perceptive remarks in Brian Willan, "Sol Plaatje, De Beers and an Old Tram Shed: Class Relations and Social Control in a South African Town, 1918 – 19," *Journal of Southern African Studies* 4, no. 2 (1978): 195 – 97.

15. Raphael Samuel, *Village Life and Labour* (London, 1975), xix.

16. This is even true of Cell's work (see n. 7), despite his attempt to include black actors in his account.

17. It is impossible to list all the relevant work here, but see for example, Charles van Onselen, *Studies in the Social and Economic History of the Witwatersrand*, vol. 1, *New Babylon*; vol. 2, *New Nineveh* (London and Johannesburg, 1982); the essays in Marks and Atmore, *Economy and Society*, and Marks and Rathbone, *Industrialisation and Social Change*; Stanley Trapido, "Landlord and Tenant in a Colonial Economy," *Journal of Southern African Studies* v, no. 1 (1978); Peter Delius and Stanley Trapido,

"Inboekselings and Oorlams: The Creation and Transformation of a Servile Class," *Journal of Southern African Studies* 8, no. 2 (1972); Colin Bundy, *The Rise and Fall of the South African Peasantry* (London, 1979); William Beinart, *The Political Economy of Pondoland, 1860 – 1930* (Cambridge and Johannesburg, 1982); Belinda Bozzoli, ed., *Labour, Townships and Protest* (Johannesburg, 1979), and *Town and Countryside in the Transvaal* (Johannesburg, 1983); Peter Delius, *The Land Belongs to Us* (London and Johannesburg, 1983); Brian Willan, *Sol Plaatje. A Biography* (London and Johannesburg, 1984), based on his "The Life and Times of Sol. T. Plaatje" (Ph.D. diss., London, 1979); David Hemson, "Class Consciousness and Migrant Labour: Dockworkers in Durban" (Ph.D. diss., University of Warwick, 1979).

18. Geoffrey Barraclough, "History and the Common Man" (Presidential Address to the Historical Association of the United Kingdom, 1966), 10.

19. Tony Judt, "A Clown in Regal Purple: Social History and the Historian," *History Workshop* no. 7 (Spring 1979), 72.

20. Gluckman, *Analysis of a Social Situation*.

21. Raphael Samuel, "People's History," in R. Samuel, ed., *People's History and Socialist Theory* (London, 1981), xxx.

22. Philip Abrams, *Historical Sociology* (Somerset, 1982), 193, 200.

23. E. P. Thompson, *The Poverty of Theory and Other Essays* (London, 1978), 280.

24. Abrams, *Historical Sociology*, xii – xv.

25. Bozzoli, *Town and Countryside*, 35.

26. This volume makes no attempt to explore the history of the Indian population of Natal, a much neglected subject. It is perhaps worth remarking how little their presence seemed to impinge on the consciousness of the subjects of these essays in the interwar period, although Dube was wont on occasion to point to the progress being made by the Indians and their relative advantages in relation to Africans, and Champion received financial assistance from Indian supporters when he first arrived in Natal. The situation was much changed after World War II.

27. Natal's secessionist posture has been splendidly satirized in Anthony Delius, *The Day Natal Took Off* (Cape Town, 1963),

while Tom Sharpe's biting novels *Riotous Assembly* (London, 1971) and *Indecent Exposure* (London, 1972) are also based on Natal's separatist traditions.

28. For the tensions over the supply of labor and criticisms of Natal's coal and sugar industries, see for example, Natal Archives, NA 191 504/F474, notes of a meeting between the prime minister and Col. Friend Addison on the subject of indenturing natives for labor, 10 May 1910; Pretoria Archives, Secretary for Native Affairs (hereafter SNA), Box 48, File 1879/744, deputation from the Mtunzini Planters Union to the minister for Native Affairs; Pretoria Archives, Government Native Labour Bureau (hereafter GNLB), 252 357/16/53, evidence before the Departmental Committee of Enquiry into the alleged shortage of native labor, Natal 1919.

Chapter 1. *The Drunken King and the Nature of the State*

1. For a similar use of ceremonial and the notion of the "imperial monarchy," see Terence Ranger, "Making Northern Rhodesia Imperial: Variations on a Royal Theme, 1924 – 1938," *African Affairs* 79 (1980): 349 – 72.

2. Chief Native Commissioner's Files, Natal Archives (henceforth CNC) 59/7/3 N/1/1/3 (32)1, Box 81. Magistrate and Native Commissioner, A. Stanford, Eshowe, to Chief Native Commissioner, Pietermaritzburg, 7 August 1930. Confidential.

3. Ibid.

4. Ibid.

5. Ibid.

6. Speeches by Native Chiefs to His Excellency, the Governor General, encl. in ibid., and Box 81, CNC 58/7/3 Stanford to CNC Pietermaritzburg, 7 August 1930, appending a report of the speech in the *Zululand Times*, 31 July 1930, with comment.

7. *ILanga lase Natal*, 29 August 1930, translated in CNC 58/7/3 29 August 1930; also Box 81, CNC 58/7/3, Stanford to CNC, Pietermaritzburg, 8 August 1930. Before Union, Africans were often punished in Natal for not offering the royal salute to *any* white man. I am grateful to Elizabeth Gunner for pointing out the

potential threat in *Bayeza* — "we (i.e. the Zulu regiments) will come" (Personal communication, November 1982).

8. Box 81 CNC 58/7/3 N1/1/3 (32) 1 A, Stanford to CNC, Pietermaritzburg , 7 August 1930.

9. Pretoria Archives, Department of Native Affairs, *Naturelle Sake* (henceforth NTS) 246 78/53 Part II, Solomon to the Resident Magistrate, Nongoma, 11 August 1930.

10. NTS 246/ 78/53 Part II, CNC, Natal to SNA, Pretoria, 7 November 1930, and minutes of an interview of the CNC, Natal, with Chief Solomon Zulu, ka Dinuzulu, at Nongoma on 22 October 1930.

11. Pretoria Archives, Department of Justice (henceforth JUS) 582 3136/31, Commissioner, South African Police, to Minister of Justice, 19 September 1930. For the significance of this meeting for the state, Champion, and the king, see chapter 3.

12. For the original report on the royal visit to Eshowe, see *Natal Mercury*, 8 June 1925.

13. Significantly the libellous article was written by Col. C. W. Lewis, who was a police officer in Zululand at the time of Dinuzulu's trial in 1907 – 8; the attack was published under the nom de plume Zitulele in the *Natal Mercury*, 13 June 1925. For the libel suit, which caused a considerable stir, see *Natal Mercury*, 6 – 13 May 1927. Solomon received £600 of the £5,000 he claimed.

14. The term *herrschaft* crept into my text subsequent to the original delivery of the Johns Hopkins lectures in response to a request for a paper to the Third International Conference on History and Anthropology, held at Bad Homburg, October 1983. I am grateful to the organizers for the opportunity I had to rethink and rework some of the original material in this chapter that was presented to that conference. The term *herrschaft* seems to me to express more adequately than either domination or authority the ambiguous relationships between ruler and ruled in Zululand that I am trying to capture, both between Solomon and "his" people and between the state and Solomon. The term still retains notions of reciprocity, *violence douce*, and obligation that are useful. As we shall see, there was rather less ambiguity in the nature of domination of the working class in Durban, and for that relationship domination is probably more illuminating than *herrschaft*.

15. *Natal Mercury* 7 May 1927. "Zulu Chief's Allegation of Libel," evidence O. Fynney.

16. For a fascinating and probably unique, if wholly unsympathetic account of the king's personal life and the meaning of a polygynous marriage for a Christian African seen through the eyes of Solomon's first wife and her feminist biographer, see Rebecca Hourwich Reyher, *Zulu Woman* (New York, 1948).

17. Box 81, CNC 59/7/3 N/1/1/3 (32)1, Stanford to CNC, 7 August 1930.

18. As Heaton Nicholls is a figure who recurs in this text, this seems a good moment to introduce some biographical detail. Born in 1876, the son of an army officer, he ran away from home at the age of fifteen to join the British army. After serving in Burma, north India, and Ceylon, whence he escorted the last of the Afrikaner prisoners of war back to Cape Town, he took service with the British South Africa Company in Northern Rhodesia. Initially he trained the Native Constabulary in Barotseland as a member of the police force; later he became a district officer. His novel *Bayete* (London, 1923) deals with those years in somewhat lurid fashion. After being made redundant in 1907, he emigrated to Australia, where after a short spell of sugar farming in Queensland, he was employed by the colonial service in Papua, where he served as assistant resident magistrate and magistrate on the gold fields at Lakekamu and Mambare between May 1910 and February 1913. His marriage to Ruby Hitchens, daughter of the Natal Minister of Railways (1906 – 10), brought him back to South Africa shortly thereafter. With his father-in-law's assistance, he started up as a sugar planter in the Umfolozi district of Zululand and rapidly rose to prominence. He became M.P. for Zululand in 1920 and played an important role in parliament in representing planter interests against the large mine owners and rose to being president of the Natal Sugar Planters and South African Sugar Planters' Associations. He was part of a South African parliamentary delegation to Canada in 1928 and advised at the Imperial Conference in London in 1931. As a permanent member of the Native Affairs Commission, he played a major role on the select committee on Hertzog's 1926 "Native bills," became a key ideologue of segregation in the United party, and hoped in

1939 to be appointed Smuts's minister of Native Affairs. In fact his marginality as an ardent proimperial Natal politician probably even more than his racial views weighed against him (although, significantly, in 1948 the Afrikaner nationalist organization, SABRA, invited him to become honorary life member), and he was dispatched instead as South African ambassador to London. After the war he became administrator of Natal, South African delegate to the United Nations, and leader of the United party opposition in the senate. He died in 1959. See his autobiography, *South Africa in My Time* (London, 1961); and Edgar H. Brookes and Colin B. Webb, *A History of Natal* (Pietermaritzburg, 1965), 269. I am grateful to Donald Denoon for additional information on Nicholls' stint in the Australian public service (Personal communication, 27 April 1978).

19. Heaton Nicholls Papers (hereafter Ms.Nic.), 2.08.1, Killie Campbell Library, Durban, KCL 3330d fragment, n.d., ca. August 1930, p. 10.

20. For the nature of production and reproduction in precolonial Natal-Zululand, see Marks and Atmore, *Economy and Society*, 9 – 20, and in the same text, Jeff Guy, "Ecological Factors in the Rise of Shaka and the Zulu Kingdom," 102 – 19; David Hedges, "Trade and Politics in Southern Mozambique and Northern Natal in the Eighteenth and Early Nineteenth Centuries" (Ph.D. diss., London, 1978). For the trade from the east coast, see Alan Smith, "The Trade of Delagoa Bay as a Factor in Nguni Politics 1750 – 1835," in L. Thompson, ed., *African Societies in Southern Africa* (Los Angeles and Berkeley, 1969).

21. Gluckman, *Analysis of a Social Situation*, 35.

22. For the self-sufficiency of the Zulu kingdom and the reasons for its conquest, see Jeff Guy, *The Destruction of the Zulu Kingdom* (London, 1979). Peter Colenbrander, "The Zulu Political Economy on the Eve of the War," in Andrew Duminy and Charles Ballard, eds., *The Zulu War. New Perspectives* (Pietermaritzburg, 1981), 78 – 97, questions the self-sufficiency, but it is clear that Zululand was, in 1879, largely outside the South African labor market. For the importance of the demand for labor in determining imperial expansion at this time, see Anthony Atmore and Shula Marks, "The Imperial Factor in South Africa in

the Nineteenth Century: Towards a Reassessment," *Journal of Imperial and Commonwealth History* 3 (1974): 1; Norman Etherington, "Labour Supply and the Genesis of South African Confederation in the 1870s," *Journal of African History* 20 (1981): 2; and N. Etherington, "Anglo-Zulu Relations, 1855 – 1878," in Duminy and Ballard, *Zulu War*.

23. For the reasons see Henry Slater, "The Changing Pattern of Economic Relationships in Rural Natal 1838 – 1914," in Marks and Atmore, *Economy and Society*, 148 – 70. For the implications for the development of the ideology of segregation in the nineteenth century and its repercussions in the twentieth century, see Shula Marks, "Natal, the Zulu Royal Family and the Ideology of Segregation," *Journal of Southern African Studies* 4 (April 1978): 20.

24. Jeff Guy, "The Destruction and Reconstruction of Zulu Society," in Marks and Rathbone, *Industrialisation and Social Change*, 167 – 94.

25. Natal Archives, 1/4/20 C 113/ 08, Krantzkop no. 1 (spy report), 14 November 1908.

26. Guy, *Destruction of the Zulu Kingdom* is by far the best account.

27. See Shula Marks, *Reluctant Rebellion. The 1906 – 8 Disturbances in Natal* (Oxford, 1970), 87 – 110.

28. CNC 57/5/4 N1/1/3 (32)1. CNC C. A.Wheelwright to SNA, Major J. B. Herbst, 17 July 1928.

29. Marks, *Reluctant Rebellion*, 238. Virtually no African women were imprisoned at this time, and the number of white males was too small to affect the numbers — so again these were mainly black males.

30. Ibid., chapters 10 and 11.

31. Although land for white occupation was set aside by the Zululand Delimitation Commission of 1902 – 5, it was really only taken into white occupation after Union.

32. For one such episode in which Solomon and one of his wives were physically attacked while visiting the mine compounds, see GNLB 213/14/9, Inspector of Native Labour, Benoni, to Director of Native Labour, Johannesburg, 3 December 1920.

33. For the hostility of his brother David, who contested Solomon's succession to Dinuzulu, and the rumors this gave rise to, see CNC

64/3 file no. 48, conf. 7, District Commandant, SAP, Eshowe to Deputy Commissioner of Police, Pietermaritzburg, 16 August 1920, and CNC 57/7/4 N1/1/3 (32)I, CNC, Pietermaritzburg, to SNA, 25 July 1932. For the continued enmity of factions of the Amandlakazi, who had spearheaded the opposition to the monarchy in the 1880s, see the same police report, and, for example, NTS 246 78/53 II, CNC, Pietermaritzburg, to SNA, Pretoria, 8 August 1930.

34. See the summary of his life in CNC 57/7/4 N1/1/3 (32)I, memo from Herbst to MNA, 15 August 1932.

35. CNC 57/7/4 N1/1/3 (32)I, CNC, Pietermaritzburg, to SNA, Pretoria, 25 July 1932.

36. Erving Goffman, *The Presentation of the Self in Everyday Life* (New York, 1959).

37. Louis R. Harlan, *Booker T. Washington: The Making of a Black Leader* (New York, 1972), viii.

38. Pretoria Archives, Native Affairs Department, NA 281/2151/F727, especially SNA to MNA 24 February 1916 and CNC, R. H. Addison, Natal, to W. Dower, Pretoria, 27 January 1916. See also ibid., notes of a meeting at the magistrate's office, Nongoma, 28 April 1916, in connection with the attempt by Solomon to hold an unauthorized hunt.

39. Ibid., CNC to SNA, 27 January 1916; E. Barrett to SNA, Cape Town, 15 February 1916.

40. Pietermaritzburg Archives, SNA, 1/955, notes of an enquiry by CNC regarding visit of David to Cetshwayo's grave, Nkandhla, 24 May 1920.

41. Ibid.

42. Box 72 CNC 57/29 N1/1/3 (32)I, CNC, Pietermaritzburg, to SNA, Pretoria, 17 August 1916.

43. Ibid.

44. For the failure of the government to purchase the farms, see Box 72 CNC 57/29, C. R. Saunders, Melmoth, to E. Barrett, Native Affairs Department, 2 October 1917. For the first of a stream of settler complaints that continued into the mid-1920s, see for example ibid., S. B. Buys, Babanango, to Prime Minister, 9 April 1917.

45 NTS 246 78/53/11, Memorandum from SNA, Herbst, to MNA,

Jansens, 15 August 1932, citing Botha, 25 November 1916.

46. Ibid., citing Wheelwright's Report, 30 November 1916.

47. The *Natal Mercury*, 18 December 1916, had little doubt that this was the reason for Solomon's reinstatement. For the administration's view, see A. M. Grundlingh, "Die Suid-Afrikaanse Gekleurdes en die Eerste Wêreldoorlog" (D. Litt. et Phil. diss., University of South Africa, 1981), 181. He cites the governor-general and the chief native commissioner for Natal as his sources. I am grateful to Dr. Grundlingh for sending me the relevant pages of his thesis. Our conclusions are very similar, although I only received his work after delivering the original Johns Hopkins lectures.

48. *Advertiser*, 3 January 1917.

49. CMT 3/930/778/2, report of O. Fynney, 9 July 1917, cited in Grundlingh, "Suid-Afrikaanse Gekleurdes," 182.

50. *Advertiser*, 25 September 1917.

51. SNA 1/4/26/1/1917, Magistrate, Estcourt, to CNC, 19 July 1917, cited in Grundlingh, "Suid-Afrikaanse Gekleurdes," 183.

52. The very considerable documentation on this is in CNC 57/7/4 N1/1/3 (32), and NTS 246 78/53/II.

53. CNC 57/7/4 N1/1/3 (32), minutes of a meeting of chief native commissioner with Solomon ka Dinuzulu (and one hundred representatives of the Usuthu chiefdom) at Nongoma on 18 February 1932.

54. Pretoria Archives, Landbou — Department of Agriculture (LDB), R2989 Magistrate, Vryheid, to Secretary for Agriculture, Pretoria, 14 December 1925.

55. CNC 64/23 N1/14/3, Wheelwright to Herbst, 23 April 1928.

56. *Natal Witness*, 15 March 1932. According to this report, women mobbed the lorries bearing famine relief maize in Mhlabatini, Nongoma, and Msinga districts. See also Box 97, CNC 68/33, replies to circular from the CNC, 22 April 1932, no. 7/1932 regarding labor supplies, which records the impact of both the drought and malaria.

57. CNC 64/23 N1/14/3 (x), CNC to Herbst, SNA, 23 April 1928.

58. See CNC 57/7/4 N1/1/3 (32), Minutes of meeting of CNC with Solomon and his followers, Nongoma, 18 February 1932.

59. I am grateful to Dr. Richard Rathbone for reminding me of the

wider comparisons.

60. See Martin Legassick, "South Africa: Capital Accumulation and Violence," *Economy and Society* 3 (1974): 3.

61. John Cell, *The Highest Stage of White Supremacy. The Origins of Segregation in South Africa and the American South*, still sees segregation as largely imposed from above, and misses the rural dimension suggested here. William Beinart, *The Political Economy of Pondoland, 1860 – 1930*, shows the significance for the shaping of the segregationist state of the attempts of chiefs to secure their authority within the colonial order, and popular demands to protect rural sources.

62. This was first presented in a set of three papers under the general title "Ideology and Social Structure in 20th Century South Africa", at the Institute of Commonwealth Studies, London, 1973. Only the last of the series was published: Martin Legassick, "Legislation, Ideology and Economy in Post-1948 South Africa," *Journal of Southern African Studies* 1 (October 1974): 5 – 35.

63. Marian Lacey, *Working for Boroko* (Johannesburg, 1981), 6.

64. Martin Chanock, *Unconsummated Union* (Manchester, 1979), 2.

65. Alf Lüdtke, "The State and Social Domination in Eighteenth and Nineteenth-Century Prussia," in Raphael Samuel, ed., *People's History and Socialist Theory*, 105.

66. Ms. Nic. 2.08.1 folder 3, pencil draft, n.d., KCM 3323.

67. Nicholls, *South Africa in My Time*, 155.

68. Pretoria Archives GG (governor-general) 1419 545/145, Memorandum by Lord Athlone, 'Certain impressions formed during the course of his tour in Zululand, 1930', 17.9.1930.

69. Ibid.

70. Native Affairs Department, *Annual Report, 1951 – 2* (Pretoria, 1955), 13.

Chapter 2. John Dube and the Ambiguities of Nationalism

1. Agnes Winifred Tucker was born in Kimberley in 1890 and studied in Cape Town, Cambridge, and Leipzig. Her first ethnographic research was carried out in the Richterveld (a part of the northern Cape region) and South West Africa. As a

teacher she taught many of the more famous younger South African anthropologists. She was married to R.F.A. Hoernle, a professor of philosophy and a prominent liberal. She died in 1960.

2. *The Star* (Johannesburg), 3 September 1934.

3. Ibid.

4. For the invitations and negotiations with African Film Productions, see CNC 57/438.

5. For Dube's life see Marks, *Reluctant Rebellion* 72 – 5, 332 – 34, 359 – 65, *passim*; Peter Walshe, *The Rise of African Nationalism* (London, 1970); R. Hunt Davies, "John L. Dube: A South African Exponent of Booker T. Washington," *Journal of African Studies* vol 2, no. 4 (Winter 1975 – 76), 497 – 528. "Ambiguities of Dependence," p. 2; W. Manning Marable, "African Nationalist: The Life of John Langalibalele Dube" (Ph.D. diss., University of Maryland, 1976).

6. *Um-Afrika*, 23 February 1946.

7. CO 179/235/22645 Governor, Natal, to Secretary of State, London, 30.5.1906.

8. Marks, "Ambiguities of Dependence," discusses the shift in white attitudes.

9. CNC 57/438, transcript of a speech by John L. Dube, 27 March 1934.

10. See for example, Magubane, *The Political Economy, Race and Class in South Africa* (New York, 1979), 57.

11. This is not to deny the profound effect that Booker T. Washington and Tuskegee had on Dube when he visited the institute in 1897. See Marable, "African Nationalist" and Hunt Davies, "John L. Dube."

12. Box 72, CNC 57/29/N/1/1/3 (32), CNC, Pietermaritzburg, to SNA, Pretoria, 17 August 1916.

13. Norman Etherington, *Preachers, Peasants and Politics in South East Africa, 1835 – 80* (London, 1978), 92.

14. John Dube, "The Need for Industrial Education in Africa," *Southern Workman* 27, no. 7 (July 1897), 142. Dube tells the same story in *A Talk Upon My Native Land* (Rochester, 1892). Although he suggests that it was Shaka who was responsible for the death of his grandfather, in fact, the regiments belonged to

Dingane, who had murdered his brother Shaka in 1828 and was himself to be displaced from the throne and killed by his younger brother, Mpande, in 1839. Lindley only arrived in Natal in 1837.

15. Bundy, *The Rise and Fall of the South African Peasantry*, 38.
16. Etherington, *Preachers*, 80.
17. Ibid., 174.
18. Ibid.,173 – 4.
19. Ibid., 118.
20. NA 254 1040/16/F596, R. Msimang to MNA, 5 July 1916.
21. Etherington, *Preachers*, 126.
22. Dube, "Need for Industrial Education," 189.
23. W. C. Wilcox, "The Story of John Dube, the Booker T. Washington of South Africa," *Congregationalist*, 10 March 1927 (cutting found in Killie Campbell Library, Durban).
24. Brian Willan, "An African in Kimberley: Sol T. Plaatje, 1896 – 8," in Marks and Rathbone, *Industrialisation and Social Change* 241 – 45, 252.
25. Cf. Anthony Hopkins, "Property Rights and Empire Building: Britain's Annexation of Lagos, 1861," *Journal of Economic History* 40 (1980): 4 — an article that sparked off many comparisons with South Africa.
26. Magubane, *Political Economy*, 55 – 6.
27. Eugene D. Genovese, *From Rebellion to Revolution: African Slave Revolts in the Making of the New World* (New York, 1981; Vintage reprint), xxi – xxii.
28. Francis Reginald Statham, *Blacks, Boers and British* (London, 1881), 186 – 87.
29. Cornelius H. Patton, *The Lure of Africa* (New York, 1917), 91 – 93.
30. CO 181/62 (17), *Natal Native Affairs Commission* (Pietermaritzburg, 1908) Annexures, pp.1005 – 6 has 1,548 landowners possessing 191,466 acres. According to the Natal Surveyor General, J. L. Masson, of this, 101,900 acres were owned absolutely, the rest still being paid for in installments. He maintained, however, that this was out of a total of 316,900 acres. (*South African Native Affairs Commission, 1903 – 5* 3: 140 – 1.)
31. Union Government (hereafter UG) 35 – 1918, Union of South Africa, *Minutes of Evidence of the Natal Natives Land Committee*, evidence of D. Sparks, Ladysmith and Klip River Agricultural

Society, October 1917, p. 36.

32. From 176,834 acres to 131,612 acres (UG 19 – 1916, *Report of the Native Land Commission* 1:5; and Lacey, *Working for Boroko*, 388).

33. *Natal Witness*, 13 February 1928.

34. UG 34 – 1918, *Report of the Local Natives' Land Committee, Natal Province*, 31.

35. GNLB 252 357/16/53 (another copy, 233/1810/F551), Natal Native Labour Shortage Committee (Interdepartmental Committee of Enquiry, unpublished), evidence taken at Stanger, p. 9.

36. UG, Native Affairs Department, *Annual Reports, 1944 – 5* (Pretoria, 1945) has a short account of the early twentieth-century history of sugar planting by Africans in Natal. There are also glimpses for the 1910s and 1920s in the annual reports to the American Board of Missions (AB) in Boston from such stations as Ifafa, Itafamasi, and Groutville. See, for example, AB 15.4, vols. 28 and 39 passim.

37. For the early Exempted Natives Society and Congress, see Marks, *Reluctant Rebellion*, 69 – 73, 358 – 63.

38. American Board of Missions (AB) (Boston), III/31/3 Letterbook, pp684 F. B. Bridgman to J. Barton, Secretary, American Board, Boston, 12 June 1908.

39. Ibid.

40. CNC 646/2, Constitution of the Natal Native Congress, 1915.

41. Mss. British Empire s19 d2/3 (Rhodes House, Oxford), dated Ohlange, 2 February 1912.

42. *Pretoria News*, 26 March 1913. Cf. "Yes, the greatest affliction of our nation is its ignorance. It is the Black man's ban [*sic*]. All his barbarism and wicked customs; all his witchcraft and superstition; all his indolence and uselessness in the labour market; all his social degradation and abject poverty; all his pathological stupidity and political misunderstanding" are attributable to lack of knowledge and education. (John Dube, *The Zulu's Appeal for Light and England's Duty* [London, 1908], 6.) One has, however, to be careful of taking this at its face value: it was very carefully contrived for the maximum effect on his missionary and philanthropic audience and designed to raise funds for his industrial school at Ohlange.

43. Leo Kuper, *An African Bourgeoisie* (New Haven, 1965), 194, cited in C.R.D. Halisi, "Black Consciousness. Ideological and Political Alignment: Notes towards an Interpretation" (paper to Social Science Research Council Joint Committee on African Studies Conference on "South Africa in the Comparative Study of Class, Race and Nationalism," New York, September 1982).

44. Magubane, *Political Economy*, 56.

45. Philip Corrigan, "Towards a History of State Formation," in Philip Corrigan, ed., *The State as a Relation of Production: Capitalism and State Formation in Marxist Theory* (London, 1980), 47.

46. Richard V. Selope Thema, "How Congress Began," in Mothobi Mutloatse, ed., *Reconstruction* (Johannesburg, 1981), 108, cited in Halisi, "Black Consciousness."

47. Stanley Trapido, "'The friends of the natives': merchants and peasants and the political and ideological structure of liberalism in the Cape, 1854 – 1910," in Marks and Atmore, *Economy and Society*, 267, 248.

48. CO 2/21, Fowell Buxton to Normanby, 20 April 1839, cited in Hopkins, "Property Rights," 796.

49. Cf. Dube, *The Zulu's Appeal*, 4 – 5, for his appeal for funds to run Ohlange in 1908. It is a frequent Dube refrain, however, designed for the Aborigines Protection Society in England and possibly also for the American philanthropists who backed him.

50. Donovan Williams, *Umfundisi. A Biography of Tiyo Soga, 1829 – 71* (Lovedale, 1979), 122.

51. ibid.

52. This paragraph and, I hope, more generally this chapter have been informed by Benedict Anderson, *Imagined Communities. Reflections on the Origin and Spread of Nationalism* (London, 1983), one of the most thought-provoking and exciting recent analyses of nationalism.

53. The phrase is Neville Hogan's in "The Posthumous Vindication of Zachariah Gqishela," in Marks and Atmore, *Economy and Society*, 277.

54. Anderson, *Imagined Communities*, 127.

55. Trapido, "Friends of the natives," 255 – 56, 268.

56. Willan, "An African in Kimberley," 244 – 52.

57. Myra Dinnerstein, "The American Zulu Mission in the Nineteenth Century Clash over Customs," *Church History*, 45, no. 2 (June 1976).
58. Etherington, *Preachers*, chap. 7.
59. Marks, *Reluctant Rebellion*, 80, see also 326 – 27.
60. Bundy, *Rise and Fall of the South African Peasantry*, 50.
61. From 46,000 in 1891 to 190,549 in 1936 (Natal Census, 1891; South African Census Report, 1936).
62. Marable, "African Nationalist," 205 – 16; and Marks, *Reluctant Rebellion*, 326 – 37.
63. American Board of Missions III/1/3 p. 409, John D. Taylor to John L. Dube, 14 September 1906.
64. Tim Keegan, "The Sharecropping Economy, African Class Formation and the 1913 Natives' Land Act in the Highveld Maize Belt," in Marks and Rathbone, *Industrialisation and Social Change*, 206. For the Land Act more generally, see Lacey, *Working for Boroko*, which deals in detail both with the 1913 Act and subsequent land legislation.
65. Keegan's "Sharecropping Economy" shows this very clearly for the Orange Free State; there has been no similarly detailed analysis for Natal, but the evidence I have seen supports this view.
66. *Natal Advertiser*, 21 February 1917.
67. Cited by Dr. A. W. Roberts before the *Select Committee on the Union Native Council Bill, Coloured Persons' Rights Bill, Representation of Natives in Parliament Bill and Natives' Land Amendment Bill*, sc19 – '27 (Union Government, 1927), 16.
68. Ibid.
69. UG 35 – '18, *Natal Natives Land Committee, Minutes of Evidence*, 38.
70. Ibid.
71. Cf. NA 315 3248/13/814, Reverend Mncadi, Roman Catholic priest, Rosebank, near Richmond, Natal, to Native Affairs Department, Pretoria, 2 May 1914:

   Protest against the man who claims himself the representative of the Native population (Mr. John Dube) and deputation to England as a mandate of the Native people when in fact it is not...Dube is not [representative]. He was elected at Free State by those who are native farmers, under the impression that

Government was going to make a bill under name Squatters Bill which would destroy the rents to those land-holders, that bill did not mention at all about separation of the races. . . . It is a pure lie to say that Mr. Dube or Native Congress as it stands represents native population but a native farming sector. The true representatives are the Chiefs of the Natives.

72. Sol T. Plaatje, *Native Life in South Africa* (London, 1916).
73. Cutting in Rhodes House, Oxford, enclosed in M. Brit. Emp. 522 G203. Unfortunately I have not been able to track down either the newspaper or the exact date, although this must have been in 1913. See also *Cape Times*, 17 March 1917, in which Dube calls the Land Act and its sister, the 1917 Native Administration Bill, "a policy of extermination."
74. UG 19 – 16, *Report of the Natives' Land Commission*, vol. 1: members of natives on various classes of land in Natal; Lacey, *Working for Boroko*, 288; and T.J.D. Fair, *The Distribution of Population in Natal* (Natal Regional Survey) vol. 3 (Department of Economics, University of Natal, Durban, n.d. [1946]), 80.
75. See n. 35 of this chapter.
76. Department of Economics, University of Natal, *Experiment at Edendale* (Pietermaritzburg, 1951), 14 – 16.
77. UG 19 – '16 *Natives' Land Committee*, vol. 1, 2 – 3.
78. United Free Church of Scotland Archives, Edinburgh, Frazer Diaries, 1924 – 25, 4: 72 – 74.
79. Cited in Walshe, *Rise of African Nationalism*, 47.
80. Philip Bonner, "The Transvaal Native Congress, 1917 – 20. The Radicalization of the Black Petty Bourgeoisie on the Rand," in Marks and Rathbone, *Industrialisation and Social Change*, 270 – 313.
81. I have obviously telescoped a great deal here. For an account of the tensions in Congress in Natal, see Walshe, *Rise of African Nationalism*, 228 – 32, 393 – 95.
82. Ibid., 42, 147. See also *Cape Times*, 17 March 1917, for Dube's involvement in large-scale land deals; and Killie Campbell Library (Durban), Oral History Project, KCAV 116 Interview, 18 March 1979, between A. Manson and A. Ncgobo, who worked on Dube's sugar plantations, where Dube "had a lot of cane under cultivation."

83. Champion papers, UCT BC 581 A1.123, Champion to Miss Frost, 16 February 1937, T (incomplete).

84. Originally published in the *New Left Review* in 1974 and republished in Nairn, *The Break-Up of Britain* (London, 1975), from which my citations are taken.

85. Nairn, *Break-Up of Britain*, 339–40.

86. See Marable, "African Nationalist," and Hunt Davies, "John L. Dube," for the voice of Booker T. Washington. "Conservative" and "moderate" are the descriptions of Dube found most generally in the older liberal and radical literature; both are but partial truths.

87. Lacey, *Working for Boroko*, 85.

88. See Shula Marks. "Natal, the Zulu Royal Family and the Ideology of Segregation," *Journal of Southern African Studies* 4 (1978): 2, n. 70, for a discussion of this point. The documents on the early formation of *Inkatha* are in the Pretoria Archives, Department of Justice, DJ 6/953/23/1.

89. Department of Justice, DJ 6/953/23/1, report of a meeting of *Inkatha* held on 8 October 1924.

90. Ibid.

91. Ibid.

92. CNC 57/7/4 N/1/1/3 (32)1, CNC, Wheelwright, to Herbst, 17 July 1928 (strictly confidential).

93. *Natal Witness*, 8 February 1928. See also Solomon's unpublished evidence before the 1930–1932 Native Economic Commission, pp.6545–6558. (The most complete set of the voluminous evidence to this commission is to be found in typescript in the library of the University of South Africa (UNISA), Pretoria. The School of Oriental and African Studies, London, has an incomplete microfilm.)

94. Natal Archives, Zulu Society files, ZS III/1/7, C. Mpanza (secretary to the Zulu Society) to H.I.E. Dhlomo, 28 December 1943.

95. Zulu Society files, ZS II/7, A. W. Dhlamini (President) to C. Mpanza, 5 January 1946.

96. *Ilanga lase Natal*, 12 August 1927.

97. See NTS 246 78/53/11, I. P. de Villiers, Commissioner of South African Police, Pietermaritzburg, to Minister of Native Affairs,

Pretoria, 19 August 1930.

98. John Foster, *Class Struggle and the Industrial Revolution. Early Industrial Capitalism in Three English Towns* (London, 1974), 5.

99. CNC 57/29 N1/1/3 (32), SNA to CNC, 20 May 1932, (private). According to Heaton Nicholls (M. Nic. 2.08.4, File 2 KCM 3833, "My Old Zululand Constituency," 23) the affair was a "fiasco," with three members of the committee engaging three different stone masons, so that the unveiling did not take place. In fact, the present monument, topped by a Greek urn and adorned with a classically inspired medallion portrait of Shaka, was unveiled at Stanger by Solomon on 1 October 1932. It is today the scene of an annual national ceremony.

Chapter 3. George Champion and the Ambiguities of Class and Class Consciousness

1. Margery Perham, *My African Apprenticeship* (London, 1978), 192.

2. For the ICU in general, see Peter Wickins, *The Industrial and Commercial Workers' Union of Africa* (Cape Town, 1978); Jack Simons and Ray E. Simons, *Class and Race in South Africa, 1950 – 1960* (Harmondsworth, 1968); Walshe, *Rise of African Nationalism*; Philip Bonner, "The Decline and Fall of the ICU: A Case of Self-Destruction?" in Eddie Webster, ed., *Essays in Southern African Labour History* (Johannesburg, 1978); Clements Kadalie, *My Life and the ICU: The Autobiography of a Black Trade Unionist in South Africa*, ed. Stanley Trapido (London, 1970); and most recently Maynard Swanson, ed., *The Views of Mahlathi. Writings of A.W.G. Champion, a Black South African* (Pietermaritzburg, 1983). Hemson, "Class Consciousness and Migrant Workers" undoubtedly has the finest and most detailed account of the ICU in Durban and in particular deals with Champion's relationship to the Durban dockworkers, in illuminating fashion, while Helen Bradford's current doctoral work at the University of the Witwatersrand is beginning to make a major contribution to our understanding of its role in rural areas. Some of her work is now appearing in print. See for example "Capitalist Development and Response to the ICU in the

Transvaal Countryside," in Bozzoli, *Town and Countryside*, 151–75; and "Mass Movements and the Petty Bourgeoisie: Social Origins of ICU Leadership, 1924–1929," *Journal of African History* 25, no. 3 (1984): 295–310. I am grateful to her for access to her unpublished papers more specifically on Natal, cited below.

3. *Udibe Lwase Afrika* (the ICU newspaper), September 1927 (found in American Board of Missions, VII/10/1).

4. Pretoria Archives, unpublished commissions (Kommissies) K22 vol. 5, ann. 133, 1929. Commission of Enquiry — Native Riots at Durban (under Commissioner C-J. de Waal, henceforth K22 vol. 5 Durban Riots Commission), p. 6. I am grateful to Paul la Hausse for helping me find the unpublished report and evidence in the Pretoria Archives, and for photocopies of a good deal of the evidence.

5. According to Champion's later account, Champion Papers, UNISA, I. 1.1. "Time is longer than the rope in the life of every man" (unpublished TSS, UNISA archives, n.d.), 1–2. This was evidently written late in Champion's life and entitled no doubt after Edward Roux's *Time Longer Than Rope* (first published 1948).

6. The phrase is Champion's own, cited in R.R.R. Dhlomo's biography, translated in Swanson, *Views of Mahlathi*, 11.

7. Helen Bradford, "Landlords, Labour Tenants and the ICU: Strikes in the Natal Midlands, 1926–8" (seminar paper, University of the Witwatersrand, 1981), 6. This apparently included migrant workers based in rural Natal.

8. K22 vol. 4, evidence to Durban Riots Commission, 12 July 1929, 440.

9. For a largely unsympathetic account of Champion's activities and the ICU in Natal, see Wickins, *Industrial and Commercial Workers' Union*, 115; Swanson, *Views of Mahlathi*, xix.

10. Many of these letters are to be found in the ICU records, A924 Champion's letterbook, Durban branch, 1925–26, in the University of Witwatersrand Archives. Their style is endearing to the contemporary reader; clearly, local employers and the Durban municipality found them less so.

11. Swanson, *Views of Mahlathi*, xx.

12. For a brilliant analysis of the use of alcohol for purposes of social control and the contradictions involved, see Charles van Onselen, "Social Control: Randlords and Rotgut, 1886 – 1903," in *Studies in the Social and Economic History of the Witwatersrand*, vol. 1, *New Babylon* (London and Johannesburg, 1982), chap. 2. For the origins of the "Durban system," its significance, and its emulation in the 1923 Urban Areas Act, see the excellent discussion in Hemson, "Class Consciousness and Migrant Workers," 129 – 40, 191 – 98.

13. K22 vol. 5, Durban Riots Commission, 3. The proportions spent on each activity are revealing: £230,209 on barracks and hostels, £217,581 on the brewery, and £19,023 on eating houses — compared with £7,681 on schools.

14. K22 vol. 1, CNC 2/47/79, CNC to SNA, Pretoria, 21 September 1929.

15. Ibid.

16. K22 vol. 5, report Durban Riots Commission, 13.

17. K22 vol. 4, evidence to Durban Riots Commission, C. W. Lewis, 3 July 1929, 24. The description of the march is reminiscent of some of the descriptions by Terence Ranger of activities of the Beni dance societies in East and Central Africa in his *Dance and Society in Eastern Africa* (London, 1975), but not nearly as elaborate. The juxtaposition of symbol is fascinating.

18. K22 vol. 5, Durban Riots Commission, 15, 22.

19. Hemson, "Class Consciousness and Migrant Workers," 205ff.

20. K22 vol. 5, Durban Riots Commission, 22.

21. Copy in JUS 6301/29 and K22 vol. 1, Magistrate Dundee to CNC, Pietermaritzburg, 19 September 1929.

22. K22 vol. 1, CNC 2/47/79, quoted in CNC to SNA, Pretoria, 21 September 1929.

23. Ibid.

24. Swanson, *Views of Mahlathi*, xxi.

25. The "token system," which still operated on the Natal coalfields, was strongly condemned by the 1930 – 32 Native Economic Commission, on the grounds that "the system is pernicious, presenting many of the features of the truck system." See *Native Economic Commission Report* (Pretoria, 1932), 139.

26. See for example K22 JUS 6301/29, District Commandant, SAP,

Natal, Dundee Division, to Deputy Commissioner, SAP, Pieter-maritzburg, 25 September 1929.

27. A.W.G. Champion, *Blood and Tears* (pamphlet in English and Zulu, n.d. [1929]) 43 (on D4683, Reel I). This militancy among African women in South Africa was not unique either to Natal or to this moment in time. Both in 1906 and in 1959 Natal women played a key role in demonstrating against the state's policies, especially in rural areas. For resistance to the pass laws by women, see Julia Wells, "Why Women Rebel. A Comparative Study of South African Women's Resistance in Bloemfontein (1913) and Johannesburg (1958)," *Journal of Southern African Studies* 10 (1983): 1.

28. The De Waal Commission into "Native Riots in Durban" (Durban Riots Commission — cited above).

29. The report of the Native Affairs Commission (at that time consisting of C. T. Loram, Senator van Niekerk, and Dr. A. W. Roberts) to the Minister of Native Affairs, 12 December 1929 (ann. 205 – '30), is in JUS 6301/29 and K22 vol. 1.

30. Ibid., Native Affairs Commission to Minister of Native Affairs, 12 December 1929.

31. None of the writers on the ICU in this period have noted the significance of the delay. Even Swanson, Champion's biographer, repeats the view that it was the "Durban riots of 1929 – 30" that "led to . . . Champion's banishment from Natal" (*Views of Mahlathi*, xxii, 31). In fact, Champion had left Durban before the "riots" of 1930, and the ICU, as we shall see, opposed the demonstrations that led to the police action in December 1930.

32. For the increased activity of the Communist party and the radicalization of the ANC, see Colin Bundy, "Land and Liberation: Popular Rural Protest and the National Liberation Movements in South Africa, 1920 – 1960," and Robert A. Hill and Gregory A. Pirio, "'Africa for the Africans': The Garvey Movement in South Africa, 1920 – 1940," both in Shula Marks and Stanley Trapido, eds., *The Politics of Class, Race and Nationalism in Twentieth Century South Africa*, (forthcoming).

33. *Star* 14 November 1929; Hemson, "Class Consciousness and Migrant Workers," 229 – 30.

34. Champion Papers, University of Cape Town, BC 581, A1,

20 November 1929. Durban beer revenues in the six months from July 1928 to the beginning of 1929 amounted to £32,000; for July 1929 to January 1930, £2000 (*Natal Mercury*, 18 March 1930, cited in Swanson, *Views of Mahlathi*, xxvi, n. 18).

35. Cf. Foster, *Class Struggle and the Industrial Revolution*, 3, for a discussion of the phenomenon in early industrial England.

36. Maynard Swanson Papers, microfilm, deposited in the Yale Collection: Native Administrative Committee Papers (copy), Rotary Club, Durban, to Town Clerk, 30 September 1929.

37. *Mayor's Minute* (Durban, 1930), found in Champion Papers, UNISA archives, acc. 1, Box 8 16.1.1, p. 10.

38. For a discussion of the concept and the use of recreation for purposes of social control, see A.P. Donajgrodzki, ed., *Social Control in Nineteenth Century Britain* (London, 1977), especially the introduction.

39. *Mayor's Minute*, 10.

40. Swanson, *Views of Mahlathi*, xxii.

41. Cited in Tim Couzens, "'Moralizing Leisure Time': The Transatlantic Connection and Black Johannesburg, 1918 – 1936," in Marks and Rathbone, *Industrialisation and Social Change*, 319.

42. The quotation from the newspaper is ca. 28 August 1929, found as a fragment on D4683 (Hoover Microfilm of ICU Papers among the Lionel Forman Papers, University of Cape Town); I have unfortunately not been able to identify it further.

43. *Mayor's Minute*, 10 – 11.

44. Swanson, *Views of Mahlathi*, xxii.

45. *Mayor's Minute*, 11.

46. Cf. Hoover Microfilm, D.4683 reel 57, Champion to Town Clerk, Durban, 27 December 1929, in which Champion expresses his gratitude at the establishment of the Native Advisory Board (NAB) and assures the town clerk of ICU cooperation "in every way"; and UNISA, Champion Papers, acc. 1 [22], Cecil Cowley to Champion, 4 November 1931, which talks of their work together as being "directly responsible" for the establishment both of the NAB and the Welfare Officer.

47. JUS 582 3134/31, Champion to Minister of Justice, 28 September 1931.

48. Natal Archives, Pietermaritzburg, Durban Corporation Archives,

Box 1617 57cc file I, Mayor of Durban to Minister of Justice, 26 September 1930.

49. According to the report of Detective Sergeant Arnold of the Criminal Investigation Department, in December 1931, the Communist party drew its 6,000 members from the ICU Yase Natal, the ANC, and Kadalie's independent ICU, with an entire branch of "the Kadalie Movement" at Clairwood going over to the party in November 1930. K22 vol. 1, Report R. H. Arnold to the Officer in Charge, CID, Durban 30 March 1930.

50. Natal Archives, Durban Corporation Archives, Box 1617A 57cc file I, report of Native Welfare Officer to Native Administration Committee, 16 January 1931. For the demonstration more generally, see Simons and Simons, *Class and Race in South Africa*, 434 – 35.

51. The number of workers in Durban declined from 30,864 in 1929 – 30 to 24,243 in 1932 – 33 (Hemson, "Class Consciousness and Migrant Labour," 265).

52. K22 vol. 1, report R. H. Arnold, 30 March 1931.

53. K22 vol. 4, Durban Riots Commission, 10 July 1929, 340. Cf. evidence of A. F. Batty before the commission, 12 July 1929, 442:

> Sergeant Arnold and I became personal friends during that trouble [when] Champion was suspended. The organisation was left entirely in the hands of subordinates. They would listen to nothing from the parent body. They wanted him reinstated at all costs. Sergeant Arnold and myself controlled the meetings. . . . the formation of the I.C.U. Yase Natal, when they seceded from the parent body, its constitution and everything in connection with the creation of that new union of natives was entirely due to the work of Sergeant Arnold and myself.

54. NTS 246 78/53/II I; P. de Villiers, Commissioner, SAP, to MNA, 19 September 1930.

55. "Time is longer than the rope in the life of every man," 4 (see note 5 this chapter).

56. NTS 78/53/II, minutes of interview of the CNC, Natal, with Chief Solomon Zulu ka Dinuzulu at Nongoma, 22 October 1930.

57. *Ilanga lase Natal*, 12 August 1927.

58. *Natal Advertiser*, 31 May 1930 (report on a meeting of the ICU).

59. NTS 246 78/53/11, Commissioner, SAP, to MNA, 19 September 1930.

60. NTS 246 78/53 part II, G. N. Heaton Nicholls to Jansen, 16 July 1930.

61. CNC 58/7/4, Herbst to Wheelwright, CNC, Natal, 7 May 1928 (personal).

62. Ibid.

63. Reyher, *Zulu Woman*, 77.

64. George Rudé, *Ideology and Popular Protest* (London, 1980), 35.

65. Shula Marks, "Class, Ideology and the Bambatha Rebellion," in Donald Crummey, ed., *Social Banditry and Rebellion in Africa*, forthcoming.

66. GNLB 252 357/16/53, evidence taken at Richmond, 31 August 1918.

67. Swanson, *Views of Mahlathi*, 22.

68. As the Native Economic Commission pointed out, it is extremely difficult to provide satisfactory wage statistics for Africans, especially when wages are provided partly in cash and partly in kind (*Report*, 131). The average at the mines is cited in the *Report*, 121, 133; the wages for the Witwatersrand are given by Ray E. Phillips, *The Bantu in the City* (Lovedale, 1939), 30 – 32. They are probably comparable, although the cost of living may have been slightly higher on the Rand than in Durban, and the figures are taken from a slightly later date. The evidence of Maj. H. S. Cooke, Director of Native Labour, and of the joint councils, is cited by F. A. W. Lucas in his Minority Report to the Native Economic Commission (*Report*, 208 – 9).

69. See for example the evidence of the Native Economic Commission, given by C. H. Wheelwright, recently retired CNC, who thought that the "Zulu in Zululand is very well off," 1742; according to G. W. Higgs, sugar and general farmer at Empangeni, "The Zulu is really a gentleman at large and he is better off than any one of us," 1768.

70. Archdeacon Lea (1914) and F. Rodseth, Superintendent Native Labour and Inspector of Native Reserves, South Zululand (1930), gave evidence to the Native Economic Commission of prosperous Zulu farmers. See also the evidence of Mkwintye, et al., Nongoma (1718ff., and 1807ff.)

71. Bradford, "Landlords, Labour Tenants and the ICU," 4.

72. *Report* SC 19 – '27 (1928), evidence of C. H. Wheelwright, 210;

evidence before the Native Economic Commission (1930 – 1932), e.g. 1612. 1664ff. Champion Papers (University of Cape Town), BC 581/B3.776, Champion to Hertzog, 24 September 1927.

73. Ibid., evidence before the Native Economic Commission, 1806 – 10.

74. Ibid., evidence before the Native Economic Commission, 1778.

75. Forman Papers, University of Cape Town, BC 581/B3.76, A. B. Ngcobo to Champion, 20 August 1927.

76. See Marks, *Reluctant Rebellion*, 86 – 87, 91, 316.

77. For the epidemic that the Natal Medical Officer of Health called a "preventible malaria disaster" in 1930, see Department of Mines and Works, MNW 798 MM 2377/25, memorandum on plantation labor in Natal, October 1925 (also ann. 452 – '26); GNLB 269/22/154, native labor on coast of Natal — methods of employment and treatment of native laborers, December-January 1922 – 23; Chief Native Commissioner, Natal, CNC 4/5 Box 16 13/2 (26); South African Railways, SAS 886 Parts I and II, G.18/17, malaria. The quotation is from Dr. G. A. Park Ross to Department of Public Health, 8 November 1930, outlining his struggles with the Railways since 1922, in SAS 886, II. I discuss the malaria epidemic in greater detail in an unpublished paper "Approaches to the History of Health and Health Care in Africa: A Tentative Offering" (African History Seminar, SOAS, London, 23 February 1983). For an illuminating parallel study of malaria in Swaziland, which brings out the close relationship between malaria, drought, and migrant labor, see Randall M. Packard, "Maize, Cattle and Mosquitoes: The Political Economy of Malaria Epidemics in Colonial Swaziland," *Journal of African History*, 25, no. 2 (1984): 189 – 212.

78. Gluckman, *Analysis of a Social Situation*, 50. Many Africans believed that the malaria was caused by whites who had poisoned the rivers (CNC 4/5 Box 16 13./2/6 (9), Superintendent of Native Reserves to CNC, Pietermaritzburg, 20 May 1932).

79. Peter Wickins, "The Industrial and Commercial Workers Union of Africa" (Ph.D. diss., Cape Town, 1973), 343 – 44; see also Kadalie, *My Life*, 159.

80. *Times* (London), 10 October 1927, cited in Wickins, "Industrial

and Commercial Workers Union," 270.

81. Bradford, "Landlords, Labour Tenants and the ICU."

82. Ibid., 12.

83. Kadalie, *My Life*, 159; Wickins, "Industrial and Commercial Workers Union," 379 – 82; *Ilange lase Natal*, 24 June 1927.

84. Margery Perham, *Ten Africans* (London, 1936), 298. It is difficult to know how far the farmers were now making use of the ICU scare to get rid of unwanted labor-tenants; as we have seen, the process of squeezing them off the farms had deeper economic roots.

85. Bradford, "Landlords, Labour Tenants and the ICU," 19 – 22.

86. In Perham, *Ten Africans*, 299 – 300.

87. Ms. Nic. 2.08.1 KCM 3348, 28 May 1929.

88. Ms. Nic. 2.08.1 KCM 3330d, carbon fragment, 10.

89. K22 vol. 4, evidence of A.W.G. Champion, 10 July 1929, 337 – 38.

90. Champion described some of his business activities to the Durban Riots Commission (ibid., 380 – 81). See also his reply to a questionnaire by M. W. Swanson, 1972, in Champion Papers, acc.1 Box 1, UNISA.

91. Swanson, *Views of Mahlathi*, xxv.

92. Forman Papers, University of Cape Town, BC 581.A1.87, Champion to H. L. Barrett, Director, Johannesburg, 27 January 1933.

93. University of the Witwatersrand, ICU Records A 924 letterbook, Champion to Laguma, 12 November 1925.

94. Hoover microfilm, D4683, Champion to Rawlins, 2 July 1930.

95. Perham, *My African Apprenticeship*, 138.

96. JUS 982 3136/1 Part I, S. J. Lendrum to Commissioner, South African Police, 17 June 1930.

97. Perham, *My African Apprenticeship*, 138.

98. Swanson, *Views of Mahlathi*, xxv. Much of this paragraph is drawn from Swanson's introduction, xxiii – xxv.

99. For this correspondence, part of it in Zulu, see Champion Papers, acc. 1 Boxes 22 and 25, UNISA. The claims about the Bantu Investment Corporation are in his letters to Chief Gatsha Buthelezi and to Senator Cecil Cowley, with whom he retained a life-long friendship as a result of Cowley's legal action on behalf of both

Champion and the ICU in the 1920s. See especially Box 25, Champion to Buthelezi, 4 September 1974. He made a similar claim to Professor Swanson in 1972 (see Swanson Questions in acc. 1 Box 1).

100. Swanson, *Views of Mahlathi*, xxv.
101. K22 vol. 5, Durban Riots Commission, 7.
102. Ibid.
103. See his interview with *Natal Witness*, 27 March 1927, cited in the Durban Riots Commission, 7, and his evidence to the commission, K22, vol. 4.
104. CNC 64/19, NC, Durban, to CNC, 23 April 1935.
105. CNC 64/19, NC, Durban, to CNC, 11 October 1935.
106. Marks, *Reluctant Rebellion*, 22.
107. GNLB 159 363/14/80, Champion to the Director of Native Labour, 22 August 1927, in which he complained of police harassment over the pass laws, which was "a source of grave injustice to the intelligent class of natives, more so to the people who have their own homes in Sophiatown, who form a better class of natives in this town."
108. Helen Bradford, "Organic Intellectuals or Petty Bourgeois Opportunists: The Social Nature of ICU Leadership in the Countryside" (African Studies Seminar Paper, African Studies Institute, University of Witwatersrand, 6 June 1983), 1. This paper was subsequently published in considerably revised form as "Mass Movements and the Petty Bourgeoisie: The Social Origins of ICU Leadership, 1924–1929," *Journal of African History*, 25, no. 3 (1984), which, however, does not contain the quotation.
109. Bradford, "Mass Movements and the Petty Bourgeoisie," 298–306. In view of the weight of racial oppression on the African "lower middle class" in this period, and the fact that "they were being forced even further from the white bourgeoisie and ever closer to the black masses," the ICU leaders "do not fit readily into schemas which stress the bourgeois nature of the petty bourgeoisie," (310). She does not, however, deny their essential ambiguity, arising out of their structurally ambiguous position between the bourgeoisie and the lower classes. See also "Organic Intellectuals," 9–11.
110. For the "deverminization," see Shula Marks and Neil Andersson,

"Epidemics and the State in Twentieth Century South Africa" (Paper to the African Studies Association of the United Kingdom and Society for the Social History of Medicine Symposium on "Epidemics and the State in Africa," 3 December 1983.

111. Report of the 5th General Missionary Council, Durban 1921.

112. K22 vol. 5, Durban Riots Commission, 4 – 5.

113. Durban Joint Council of Europeans and Natives, 1931, "Report of Committee to investigate and report on health of Durban Natives" (n.d. [ca. 1931]), 4. (From South African Institute of Race Relations, Reinhallt-Jones Papers, Joint Councils -D, University of Witwatersrand.)

114. Bonner, "Transvaal Native Congress," 289.

115. Hemson, "Class Consciousness and Migrant Labour," 167 – 87.

116. For the enmity between Champion and Dube, see BC 581 b4.80, Exercise Book: Draft of a letter to *Ilange lase Natal*, in which Champion remarks, "Our history with Dube is bitter. My sin in his eyes is that I came to Natal to blot out his name by organising the ICU and destroyed his stronghold Durban" (May 1928). The enmity continued with more or less bitterness until Dube's death in 1946.

117. See for example NA 191 504/F474, notes of a meeting between the Prime Minister and Col. Friend Addison on the subject of indenturing natives for labor, 10 May 1910; Pretoria Archives, Secretary for Native Affairs, SNA Box 48 file 1879/744, deputation from the Mtinzini Planters Union to the Minister for Native Affairs; Pretoria Archives, GNLB 252 357/16/53, evidence before the Departmental Committee of Enquiry into the Alleged Shortage of Native Labour, Natal 1919; and ann. 268 – '26, *Labour Conditions on the Sugar Estates, Natal.*

118. For Gandhi and the 1913 strike, see Maureen Tayal, "The 1913 Indian Strike in Natal," Journal of Southern African Studies 10. no. 2 (April 1984): 239 – 58.

119. Wickins, *Industrial and Commercial Workers' Union*, 145.

120. Hoover microfilm, D4683, reel I, evidence to the South African Native Economic Commission, March 1930.

121. According to the missionary J. D. Taylor at the 5th General Missionary Council, Durban, 1921, 3.

122. Bradford, "Mass Movements and the Petty Bourgeoisie," 296,

300, 309. My interpretation of Champion's actions here owes a great deal to this splendid article.

123. Hemson, "Class Consciousness and Migrant Labour," 6.

124. Champion recalls these episodes, as well as subsequent episodes of unequal confrontation, in "Time is longer than the rope in every man's life," p. 14, Champion Papers, UNISA, acc. 1, Box 1.

125. Interview with Tom Karis, 25 March 1964. I am grateful to Professor Karis for a copy of the transcript.

126. Perham, *Ten Africans*, 305.

127. Hoover microfilm, D4688 reel I, Champion to President and the Governing Body of the ICU Yase Natal, 24 February 1930.

128. Ibid.; see also *Natal Advertiser*, 31 May 1930, report of a meeting of the ICU.

129. JUS 582 3136/31 Part I and K22 vol. 1, S. J. Lendrum to Commissioner, South African Police, Pretoria, 17 June 1930.

Chapter 4. Conclusions

1. Nicos Poulantzas, *Political Power and Social Classes* (London, 1973), 203.

2. See for example, E. J. Hobsbawm, *Primitive Rebels* (Manchester, 1959); and George Rudé, *Ideology and Popular Protest*, 32.

3. Gluckman, *Analysis of a Social Situation*, 22, 43-44.

4. The phrases are from Anderson, *Imagined Communities*, 40, 13 (respectively).

5. Elizabeth Colson, "Contemporary Tribes and the Development of Nationalism," in June Helm, ed., *Essays on the Problem of Tribe. Proceedings of the 1967 Annual Spring Meeting of the American Ethnological Society* (Seattle, 1968).

6. Unfortunately there has been no study of Stuart's role in the creation of Zulu history. Colin de B. Webb and John Wright have, however, brought out three volumes of his oral interviews on Zulu history (see *The Stuart Papers* [Pietermaritzburg, 1978 – 82]). There are still two to follow. His readers on Zulu history include *uVusezakithi, uHlangakhula, uLaxoxele, uKwesukela, uThlasizwe,* and *uVulingqondo.* By the 1930s they were widely used by the Natal Education Department and published by Longmans Green, London. For Stuart's views on the

dangers of "detribalization" see Hemson, "Class Consciousness and Migrant Labour," 112 – 13.

7. As Maurice Godelier shows in "The Non-Correspondence between Form and Content in Social Relations: New Thoughts about the Incas," in his *Perspectives in Marxist Anthropology* (Cambridge, 1977), 186 – 96.

8. Ernesto Laclau, *Politics and Ideology in Marxist Theory* (London, 1977), 157.

9. Gluckman, *Analysis of a Social Situation*, 15.

10. The accusation that Harrison Wright levels against liberal and radical historians of South Africa alike, in his *Burden of the Present: Liberal-Radical Controversy over South African History* (Cape Town, 1977).

11. *History Workshop*, Editorial Collective, "Editorials" 1, no. 1 (1976): 2.

12. *Buthelezi Commission on the Requirements for Stability and Development in KwaZulu and Natal* (henceforth *Buthelezi Commission*) (Durban, 1982), "Report of the Economic Sub-Committee," 2: 135.

13. In 1980, about 46 percent of the approximately six million Zulu were in Kwazulu; most of the rest were in Natal. The terms *de jure* and *de facto* refer to the numbers actually in Kwazulu and those whom the government assigns to Kwazulu as their "homeland" — even though they may have been living in Durban or Johannesburg for their entire lives.

14. South African Institute of Race Relations (SAIRR), *Survey of Race Relations in South Africa, 1982* (Johannesburg, 1983), 412.

15. *Buthelezi Commission*, 1: 81.

16. Liz Clarke and Jane Ngobese, *Women without Men* (Durban, 1975).

17. *Buthelezi Commission*, 2: 146, 156 – 57.

18. SAIRR, *Survey of Race Relations in South Africa, 1982*.

19. One can do no more than estimate infant mortality because the South African state does not collect statistics on the diseases of malnutrition and there is no national register of African births and deaths. Although infant mortality has dropped among coloureds in Cape Town and Africans in Soweto, indications from the rural areas suggest a rate as high as 200 to 250 per 1,000. For the

effects of malnutrition, see World Health Organization, *Apartheid and Health* (Geneva, 1983), 108 – 12, 141 – 63.

20. *The Buthelezi Commission*, 2: 128.

21. "Conference of Eight Black Leaders with the Hon. Adv. B. J. Vorster and the Honourable Mr. M. C. Botha, MP (Cape Town, 22 January 1975), 56 (typescript, marked confidential).

22. *Buthelezi Commission*, 1: 77 – 78.

23. Mangosuthu Gatsha Buthelezi, "Independence for the Zulus," in N. J. Rhoodie, *South African Dialogue* (New York, 1972).

24. *The Constitution of the National Cultural Movement of Inkatha* (as amended) (n.d., n.p.), chap. 1, paragraph 1 (lithograph).

25. For *Inkatha*, see Roger Southall, "Buthelezi, Inkatha and the Politics of Compromise," *African Affairs* 80, no. 321 (October 1981): 453 – 81. The figures are on p. 455.

26. "Speech by Mangosuthu G. Buthelezi on the opening of Mr. Edward Ngobese's Supermarket, Kwadlangubo Trading Centre, Eshowe, 5 August 1977," 6.

27. cf. "The rate at which unemployment is rising might just be that spark that will ignite that powder-keg" (ibid., 10).

28. Southall, "Buthelezi, Inkatha and Compromise," 458.

29. See for example John S. Saul and Saul Gelb, "The Crisis in South Africa. Class Defence, Class Revolution," special issue of *Monthly Review* 33, no. 3 (1981): 91ff.

30. For an excellent discussion of the tensions in this relationship, see John D. Brewer, "Inkatha: A Preliminary Anatomy" (unpublished paper, 1980). I am grateful to John Brewer for allowing me to see this prior to the publication of his book on *Inkatha*.

31. "13th Mafukuzela Week: Dr. John Langalibalele Dube: Statesman, Sage, Scholar and Leader — His Achievements and the Lessons of These to Us in the Struggle for Our Own Liberation," address by the Hon. Prince M. G. Buthelezi, 5 May 1974, mimeographed (author's copy).

32. Ibid., 2.

33. See for example, SAIRR, *Survey of Race Relations in South Africa, 1983* (Johannesburg, 1984), 346.

34. "Natal Education Boycott: A Focus on Inkatha," *Work in Progress*, no. 15 (October 1980, Johannesburg).

35. "Conference of Eight Black Leaders," 59.

36. Cited in SAIRR, *Survey of Race Relations in South Africa, 1983*, 346.
37. Saul and Gelb, *Crisis in South Africa*, 127.
38. Elizabeth Gunner, "Ukubonga Nezibongo: Zulu Praising and Praises" (Ph.D. diss., University of London, 1984), chap. 2, p. 14. I am grateful to Liz Gunner for showing me this in draft form.
39. Ibid., 18.
40. Brewer, "Inkatha: A Preliminary Anatomy."
41. Saul and Gelb, *Crisis in South Africa*, 127.
42. *Economist*, 13 March 1982.
43. Saul and Gelb, *Crisis in South Africa*, 127.
44. This is supported by the work of Elizabeth Gunner on Zulu praise poetry, which suggests that much Zulu speech is "oblique: the meaning is not obvious on the surface, but can be deduced by those who are in the know. . . . the praise poetry uses this allusive, elliptical style a lot. It can become a kind of code and the *imbongi* (praise poet) varies the degree of difficulty of the code" (personal communication from Elizabeth Gunner, 1 November 1982).

Index

The letter *q.* indicates quoted material.

Study of indivs offers us a way
of getting at historical issues + realities.
For what is point of history?

Getting at why someone acts a way —
motives — helps us understand. But so
elusive + ambig — even to them.
                                              colon.
Ambig + ID critical to understanding of Afr.
& other cross-cultural work?

How can indiv ambig/ID's inform more
[general/structural approaches?
& what are goals of history?
[Colon./Eur. ambigs — how infl. by Afr's]
↳ method of expl: Glass,
 — explanatory strengths + weaknesses of
   each; explanat. of what?

Nature of indirect rule — give credence
to local structure — colon. interest not in
form (educ., dress, lang etc.) but in substance —
did this behav. allow them to get rich?

Diff's in colon. frameworks — Engl., settler,
admin, econ. (busin., relig. — diff. motives.
Role of state — theory? Vs. capital.
Behind motives: expl's of structure, indiv. hist,